EO DC

JACK DALY WORKSHOP

MAY 3, 2022

COMPLIMENTS OF

OUR STRATEGIC ALLIANCE PARTNERS

PAT BRAUNSCHEIDEL
M&T BANK

ROY MORRIS
DUNLAP BENNETT & LUDWIG

NEMA SEMNANI
PRECISION SALES CONSULTING

JOE CHAPMAN
DANAHER-SKEWES & ASSOCIATES, INC.

MICHAEL SAVAGE
BANK OF AMERICA PRIVATE BANK

JIM GIANINY
VERITAS SOLUTIONS

GREG PACKER
ACCESS POINT

STEVE KENNEY
CHERRY BEKAERT

GREG MCDONOUGH
CHAPTER PRESIDENT

EODCNETWORK.ORG

PRAISE FOR
JACK DALY'S LIFE BY DESIGN

"Very quickly I learned that Jack is very intentional about what he spends his time on and what he does not spend his time on. I still vividly remember the first time I heard him say, 'We all have 168 hours in the week; it's up to you to decide how you use them.' This statement changed my life, personally and professionally.

I started learning from Jack how to have the hard conversations up front with my boss, my sales reps, and my wife so I could start focusing on only the things I needed to do in order to achieve the goals I wanted to achieve personally and professionally. His processes helped me determine what the high-value activities are that I need to focus on, and what other activities I need to stop doing. He uses systems and processes for everything and then measures if he is getting the results he wants from them.

When I met Jack, I was a sales manager for a small foundation-repair company on pace to sell $11 million that year with about twelve salespeople. I was married and had two young kids. I had what I wanted, I owned my own home, I had the family I always wanted, and I had a steady job. But something was missing. My wife and I weren't as happy as we thought we would be. Why were we not happier when we had what we wanted? The answer was that we were 'disorganized' in our life. I was trying to toe the line of 'work/ life' balance. We were sharing responsibilities with the kids and never able to keep up at home or at work. She and I were not able to focus on our careers and run our household the way we wanted it to run.

After the first time I heard Jack, I realized both my wife and I were spending time on things we were not good at or didn't enjoy, just because we thought we needed to 'share all responsibilities.' I quickly learned from Jack and his systems and processes that you focus on the things that get you what you want and remove the rest.

My wife and I were able to divide where we spend our time and what we spend our time on. She ended up quitting her full-time job and focusing on running the house. In order to do that financially, we needed me to be more successful at work and earn more income. So I focused on work. I cut out anything that didn't drive toward my goal. I was able to hire people to take over things that were important but not important for me to do. I was able to afford hiring these people by increased productivity when I didn't spend my time on things that didn't drive toward my goals.

Fast-forward a few years later, and I am the director of sales of the same company, on pace to sell over $30 million, managing over thirty sales reps, plus a service team of ten people. I am able to see most of the kids' baseball games, dance recitals, and tae kwon do competitions. We are able to take several vacations a year. My wife is happier, my boss is happier, and I am happier, all because I chose to start living a life by design. Jack's systems and processes work both personally and professionally. At our company we have a motto: discipline = freedom. Jack and his processes exemplify that motto."

—**Mark Steiner,** Director of Sales, Dry Pro Foundation and Crawlspace Specialists, Charlotte, NC

"Jack is one of the most unique and special professionals you're ever going to meet … his energy and enthusiasm are only matched by his approach to the big issues in business and life that create actionable, effective, and relatively simple solutions.

Jack Daly's artful and colorful language and examples are certain to connect in a powerful and memorable fashion that drives real, durable value. I recommend Jack Daly's books, speaking, and methods to any person who is interested in benefiting from the countless lessons of a life most purposefully well lived."

—**Mike Ferranti,** Founder and CEO, BuyerGenomics Technologies

"Thank God Jack Daly exists! For decades, we hired Jack to teach us how to sell better, yet, all the while, what he was actually teaching us was how to be better human beings. Most of us have wondered about how he got to be the way he is (with the hope we can try to be even a fraction more like him). This is the book that tells us … and anyone who wants to be a better version of themselves needs to read it!"

—**Simon Sinek,** Optimist and *New York Times* Best-Selling Author of *Start with Why* and *The Infinite Game*

"At a quick glance, it is clear that Jack is a powerful and inspiring speaker and author. This book gives us a look under the hood of the supercharged Jack Daly engine. Upon closer inspection, we learn that we are witnessing the by-product of a deliberate conscious life, a life by design. Our own versions are available for all of us with a commitment to consistent practice and growth. Jack is a gift for us all that just keeps on giving."

—**Tony Lillios,** lillios.com: Personal and Professional Coaching; Parks California: building access and stewards to California State Parks

"Jack Daly is the most important mentor that I have had in my fifty-five years (and I have had many). The way Jack shows up consistently each and every day of his life coupled with the planning/setting goals/measuring them and holding yourself accountable both professionally and personally *always* is a recipe for everyone to succeed, period. I continue to suggest to anyone I know in business or budding young entrepreneurs: 'Get to know Jack Daly, and follow his plan!' I am grateful for the success I have had in *all* areas of my life and attribute much of this to the incredible sage Jack. Buy this book for everyone you know that needs some assistance on how to achieve success, and if they read it and follow the principles, they will succeed guaranteed!"

—**Jody Steinhauer,** President and Chief Bargain Officer, bargains-group.com

"There simply isn't a bucket big enough to hold everything on Jack Daly's list. Watching Jack achieve in business, in his personal life, and in sports has been more than humbling; it's been an education. Want to crush your bucket list? Grab a copy of Jack's book, and prepare to learn from the master."

—**G. Michael Maddock**, Serial Entrepreneur, Author, and Public Speaker

"As Jack often says, 'the tale of the tape' tells the story of how his work has affected our business and my life.

Using what I learned, we catapulted our company to five times our industry profitability, over two hundred people, six acquisitions, and made our investors a mint! Along the way, I got to see a lot more of Jack, becoming a valued friend, fellow triathlete, challenger, and confidante.

Jack also challenged me to push myself personally and physically with great benefit. With Jack's challenging and encouraging, I now have completed three full Ironman races and countless other shorter-distance events."

—Richard Manders, Cofounder, FreeScale Coaching Systems

"I persistently messaged him every time I saw he was in town. I said I'd take him to dinner, meet him wherever he wanted, carry his bags … whatever it took! He finally accepted my invitation to drive him to the airport. I was ecstatic because I wanted to thank him for planting a life-changing seed.

I had just started my alcohol recovery after accepting my unhealthy choices couldn't continue. Fueled by Jack's story, I had signed up and finished the Ironman Florida triathlon—something that was way outside my comfort zone. All I knew was that I was finally on the right path—a path that Jack inspired.

We've since become great friends. We've crossed the Grand Canyon on foot together. We've finished the NYC marathon side by side to raise money for cancer research in Bonnie's name. So many laughs and tears along the way. I can't put into words how much Jack means to me. He's a friend, mentor (I often think 'What would Jack do in this situation?'), and one of my favorite people of all time.

So when I heard he's writing a book on lifestyle design, I instantly knew we're all in for a treat. You see, Jack knows how to set goals at the next level. He is a master at building systems and processes to maximize his time on this planet and impact everyone around him.

I hope you all digest this book and, as Jack says, 'take action!' If you do, I know you'll look back on your full life with no regrets."

—James Ashcroft, Business Coach

"He's made an indelible impact on me. Personally, in my business, and in my life. Flat out—Jack's ideas ring true, and they work. He's been an unparalleled driving force behind my motivation and success.

Anyone that knows Jack knows he has always lived a remarkable life, on his terms. We can learn priceless lessons from someone who has excelled at this all his life.

His playbook to live life by design is a roadmap to grab your life by the horns. It's an inside look at how to create a meaningful life that you want, on your terms. To live the life you hope to live.

Like a true friend, Jack tells it like it is. He lights the path to 'suck more juice out of life,' as he says. He builds an infectious desire to get more out of life. This is life success by design.

Study it. Sharpen focus. Take immediate action, backed with passion. Then measure what matters most to live the life of your dreams."

—**Dan Larson,** Coauthor *The Sales Playbook for Hyper Sales Growth*; CEO of LeverageSalesCoach.com Coaching Company and LeveragePlaybook.com

"*Buy this book!!* Let me explain. I am pretty sure that I have read all of Jack Daly's books. They have each made a significant impact on my business and personal life, particularly relating to sales and leadership. This book is a bit different. It focuses on the big picture—living your life by design, something most of us rarely do. I have known Jack for over twenty-five years. He is not only a tremendous author and speaker, but he is a true inspiration, living each day of his life to the fullest, all by design … Jack Daly accomplishes more in a quarter than most people do in a lifetime. And he seems to do it all with passion and enthusiasm rarely seen. I'm exhausted each quarter from simply reading his incredible list of accomplishments. If you want to live a life by design, you'll want to read this book and get started right away."

—**Jeff Dennis,** Lawyer, Serial Entrepreneur, and Best-Selling Author of *Lessons from the Edge*

"It is life changing. Jack has given us a step-by-step guide on how to live life. I love every part of this book—from the early years to life's surprises to how he sets his personal goals. Jack is right—'routine does set you free'—and he shows you how to do this. Jack lives this every single day and is an inspiration to thousands around the world. There are many pearls of wisdom in this book that will change the trajectory of your life."

—**Maria Padisetti,** CEO, Digital Armour Corporation

"I can say from personal experience, Jack Daly is a true entrepreneur with one volume and a spirit and drive unlike anyone you'll ever meet. I've worked with Jack for several years now growing my own branding and marketing firm, and I owe so much of our 'sales' success directly to Jack's expert guidance. When Jack makes an introduction, it is thoughtful and intentional and will no doubt be a match. His skill to understand his colleague's personality, professional goals, and business needs is outstanding. He even knows me better than myself at times! Jack is truly a gem, and I am thrilled to call him a partner and a friend."

—**Fran Biderman-Gross,** CEO and Founder of Advantages; Coauthor of *How to Lead a Values-Based Professional Services Firm: 3 Keys to Unlock Purpose and Profit*; Public Speaker; and Producer of the Podcast *Drive Profit with Purpose*

"On the surface, Jack Daly can be a bit intimidating. How can anyone be so successful? His accomplishments seem superhuman and, therefore, unattainable to the rest of us mere mortals. Write him off … at the risk of your own success.

He's been my client, my customer, and, through it all, my friend. Jack is generous, principled, and caring. Exceptionally disciplined. And wicked smart! He is living proof of what's possible."

—**Marilyn Murphy,** Founder and "Creative Queen" of The WOW! Travel Club, marilyn@wowtravelclub.com

"If Jack Daly scribbled on a piece of paper, I'd want to read it. Jack is pure GOLD—he's the real deal and knows how to get the results he's after! He shares easy-to-follow processes anyone can and should put into practice to redirect their lives overnight. *A must read!*"

—**Martin Grunburg,** A uthor of *The Habit Factor*® and *The Pressure Paradox*™

"Meeting and becoming friends with Jack has been a blessing and a curse; let me explain.

As a thirty-two-year-old magician who travels the world 'turning tricks,' I can happily say Jack and his process have changed my life for the better. Every time I see myself facing a goal I'd like to achieve, I think to myself 'What would Jack do?' And the answer seems to magically appear!"

—**Denny Corby,** Comedy Magician

"Jack is the master at living life on his own terms, doing the things he loves most, and always sharing with his friends and family. I continue to learn from Jack 'daly' and look forward to sharing his book with many!!"

—**Howie Kra**

"Rarely do we meet a true role model who inspires so many people in so many areas of life from goal setting to healthy living to relationships to business success (and more). In this book, Jack details how he lives his life by his design and how others can too. His personal stories are serious yet told in a lighthearted, humorous way—a pleasure to read. I laughed out loud when young Jack created, then owned the 'pot holders made by boys' market … a brilliant use of sales language to spike growth! I wholeheartedly recommend this book as a must read for those who want to live their best lives!"

—**Caryn Kopp,** Chief Door Opener, Founder of Kopp Consulting's Door Opener® Service, and Coauthor of Best Seller *Biz Dev Done Right*

"I have had the pleasure of knowing Jack Daly for over twenty years. In my thirty-five years of business, I have never met anyone that has the passion, discipline, and talent to positively impact tens of thousands of people not only by his words but, more importantly, by his actions. I had the honor of being invited to celebrate Jack's seventieth birthday by hiking the Grand Canyon in what is known as Rim2Rim2Rim. This entails hiking twenty-five miles in one day and hiking back the very next day twenty-five miles, which takes on average twelve hours a day. This was one of the five hundred bucket list items for Jack to accomplish. Although I only was able to do Rim2Rim with delight, Jack was able to complete the fifty-mile hike with many of his friends that are twenty years his junior. His fanaticism in preparation and how he does the little things is how he does the big things. This is a classic example of Jack Daly not only talking the talk but 'walking the walk.'

If you want to accomplish things outside of your comfort zone and learn the process and systems of doing things that model the masters, I highly encourage you to read *Jack Daly's Life by Design*."

—**Devin Schain,** Serial Entrepreneur and Philanthropist

"Jack Daly gave me the insight, process, system, and inspiration to 'be' better and more focused than I ever thought possible. I began my own *Life by Design* journey many years ago and have actively pursued big personal and professional goals with Jack's 'calendar' as the basis for it all. I have publicly spoken hundreds of times about my own success and process for achieving greater and greater goals by applying focused effort and following a process. This book, alongside Jack's insight, will give you what you need to do the same if you will simply take it and apply as I have. Thank you, Jack, for giving me my own start and for writing this book to show others what is possible!"

—**Andy Bailey,** Founder of Petra Coach; Author of *No Try Only Do* and *Vitamin B for Business*

"I've taken Jack's seminars and have read all his books. I view him as my life and sales mentor. Applying Jack's life's principles as my own have helped me stay focused on what I want out of life and my career.

I can honestly say that I am living proof that you can achieve life by design. I'd recommend listening to or reading anything Jack says or writes. His advice is as good if not better than gold."

—**Ileana Landon,** Director of Radio and Podcasting, North America-Megatrax Production Music

"The stories he shared and the insight he imparted on how to not only build and scale highly successful businesses but how to truly live his life to the fullest were what really struck me.

Many people would consider the life that my wife, Irina, and I lead to be insanely busy; they would not consider us to be slouches when it comes to our approach to living life to its fullest. But when compared to the life that Jack lives—he is on a whole different level.

Through his mentorship, I learned the strategies he uses to maximize the impact that he makes and, perhaps most importantly, the shift in mindset that I needed to make in order to truly lead an exceptional life. This has led to substantial growth of my business as we expanded across Canada, building stronger relationships with amazing people around the globe, and a more fulfilling home life built on the foundation of purpose and significance that has enhanced the bond that I have with my family.

If you're looking to take your business, your relationships, and your life to the next level, Jack's book is a *must read* to learn the processes, strategies, and mindset you need to have in place to truly live your life to the fullest!"

—**Vincent Fung,** Managing Director and CEO, www.experaIT.com

"Want to be inspired? Learn Jack Daly's story by reading this book. Jack works hard and gets results. Jack has incredible energy and loves to teach others how to live a life of purpose. This book is a must read for anyone who wants to understand how to get results."

—Joe Apfelbaum, CEO of Ajax Union

"I have made many changes inspired by our time together. I have lost sixty-five pounds, in spite of COVID-19 and needing knee replacements. Income and opportunities have more than doubled; I have a keen sharpness of focus on what matters most. My goals are written and measurable. Thank you for continuing to be an inspiration."

—John Papaloukas

"I went to my first Jack Daly sales seminar in 1997, and ever since I've been a disciple of Jack's wisdom, gratitude, and incredible self-discipline when it comes to living a full and enriched life. Over the years, I have tried to apply his insights and methodologies to all facets of my life, and any successes I've managed to accomplish are ultimately a direct result from applying Jack's philosophies and teachings in both my business and personal life."

—Jim Kalb, President, Triad Components Group

"Am blessed to run his last state marathon together with him in New Jersey in October 2018. He is a man of great vision, humor, passion for life, and a true friend. He inspires anyone he meets, captivates them telling stories, and life becomes better with him."

—Burak Alpaslan, Certified Financial Planner, Vegan Ironman Triathlete

"Ever since meeting Jack through the EO university in Japan fourteen-plus years back, I have been a huge fan of his work. He has taught me more through his classes and lectures as well as his books than anyone I have heard speak at the organization. We have had a lot of amazing speakers over the years, so that is a pretty strong statement. With his guidance and support and knowledge, I have personally become the largest salesperson in an industry with over a couple hundred thousand salespeople. Aside from the sales side of what I learned from him, the pure discipline has also been instrumental in making me who I am today. Thank you, Jack, for everything you have taught me. I hope more people can take what you have taught me and apply it to their own industry and world."

—**Brett Marz,** Cofounder of BAMKO

"I had the opportunity to see Jack Daly speak many years ago at an Entrepreneur Organization event and immediately said to my peers, 'This guy speaks my language.' At that time, I would never have known the impact he would have on me and my business. On the business side he brings unbelievable energy with years of experience in sales to help your sales team grow. On the personal side Jack truly lives his motto of *Life by Design*, and no one can match his annual goals and bucket list. Over the years I have had the pleasure of joining Jack to run marathons, hike the Grand Canyon, and share many conversations on life and goals. This book is a must read for people looking to get the most out of their life."

—**Andy Heck,** President and Co-Owner, AlpinHaus

"I've known Jack well for over twenty years now—and watched him literally rip the cover off the ball of life. You'll want everyone you know to read this book to have as much fun and success in life as he has. We only live once, and he shows us how to really live it."

—**Cameron Herold,** Founder and COO of Alliance; Author of *Vivid Vision*

"Jack Daly is my drug of choice. I'm always Jack'd up! Nothing else on this planet can get me pumped up and ready to attack the world like Jack can. His energy is massively contagious. If you want to reach and surpass your God-given potential, read this book, read Jack's other books, and follow him on social media."

—**David Mammano,** Growth Specialist, Host of *The Gonzo Experience* podcast

"If you don't design your life, it will be designed by others.

It takes courage to live life by design. Courageous people overcome the fear of failure that accompanies bold dreams. Courageous people share their bold dreams with others. Courageous people create plans with milestones, time frames, and resources so they can track their progress and adjust the trajectory of their decisions. Courageous people learn how to improve their chances of success.

If you have the courage to pursue happiness on your own terms, study *Jack Daly's Life by Design*."

—**Mark Rubin,** Builder

"I've known Jack Daly for over thirty-five years. Here is a man who sets his goals in December (lofty ones, I might add!) and then attacks and achieves them. I love that his goals encompass the bastions of life: family, health, exercise, love, and fun. He is a standard I try to live up to in living my life by design."

—Billie Attaway, Recovering Entrepreneur

"Learn from the best. I first met Jack at a YPO seminar. Since then, I have been very fortunate to have developed a unique friendship with Jack; without sounding patronizing, the man is truly remarkable on so many levels. He just gets it and says it how it is. No BS! Even when using an f-bomb to highlight something of utmost importance, his delivery is powerful, his comments thought provoking, and he is just a great guy, and I'm happy to call him a close friend and mentor."

—Jeff Shavitz, CEO, ToolBox Payment

"I have known Jack Daly since 1994. We have been business partners and great friends and have experienced many bucket list items together. I have watched him firsthand live life to the fullest every single day at everything he does. He has lived the life that many only dream of by building the life he wants by design. Read this book, and you can get inspired to do the same."

—Mark Moses, CEO and Founding Partner, CEO Coaching International; Author of *Make BIG Happen*

"I first met Jack Daly as a CEO National Account client in 1987 when I was an executive at a General Electric Co. subsidiary. Fortunately for me, we have stayed connected consistently ever since. He is truly the most amazing, dynamic, energizing, inspiring, goal-focused, accomplished, and fun person I have ever known. His story from childhood all the way through his professional career path is an absolute must read. His vast accomplishments and life adventures will have you questioning how this could all be true. Trust me; it is all true and not embellished—plus he always walks his talk. This man has positively impacted literally thousands of lives, and I am confident every reader of this book will be counted among them."

—Theodore A. "Ted" Miller

"Jack Daly is a living legend of the power of goals, passion, and purpose. He lives what he teaches, demonstrates daily what he shares, and inspires everyone around him to be the best version of themselves. Jack has designed a life that most people dream of having one day, and yet he lives it every day! If you only read one book this year, it must be this book!"

—Keith Abraham, CSP, Founder of Passionate Performance

"If you can take just a fraction and implement what Jack says and does in this book and in life, you will be handsomely rewarded spiritually, emotionally, and materially. Jack is the real deal, so don't just put the book down when you finish it; live it."

—Jim Moularadellis, Friend

"'You get what you measure!' I've never known a human being that more exemplifies this philosophy than Jack Daly. I have found that when you follow Jack's formula, success in business and life is simple."

—Patrick Condon, FBC Remodel and The Joy Formula

"Jack speaks to the core of your soul like no other. The impact of Jack's wisdom on my life is comparable to having children … it's a freaking game changer. Jack convinced me to quit talking about being exceptional and just commit to putting a plan in place. Reader, beware; once you taste how extraordinary your life can be, there's no going back."

—**Shay Eskew,** Thirty-five-time Ironman Finisher on Six Continents; Best-Selling Author and Motivational Speaker; National Wrestling Hall of Fame Inductee

"Anyone who wants to create bigger and more purposeful impact with their life needs to read Jack's book! Jack is *the* example of someone who lives life with intention and passion. Learning from Jack will leave you inspired and thinking *big*. In addition, Jack's tools and methods are easy to implement and provide awesome results! I have been a student of Jack's for years, and his tools have been critical in helping me build my companies and create a life with bigger impact and purpose. I sure am grateful I got to know Jack!"

—**Barrett Ersek,** CEO and Founder, Holganix

"Jack's ability to see and plan his future at the age of thirteen is nothing short of astonishing. The story of his early years has takeaways for everyone. His determined passion and focus on his 'Why' and his resulting achievements are as instructional as they are inspirational. This book should go to the top of anyone's reading list that wants to make highly impactful changes in their life."

—**P. Allan Young Jr.,** Founder and Chairman, FranBridge Capital

"Michael Gerber, author of *The E-Myth*, taught me how to systematize my business. My friend Jack Daly showed me how to systematize my life! A goal without a plan is just a wish. And Jack never wishes … he makes goals happen! Thank you, Jack, for the inspiration!"

—**Brian Scudamore,** Founder and CEO of 1-800-GOT-JUNK? and O2E Brands; Author of *WTF?! (Willing to Fail): How Failure Can Be Your Key to Success*

"I first met Jack in Kona, Hawaii, in 2006 on the eve of my first Half Ironman, in which we were both competing. This was the next-to-last step in my publicly stated goal of completing a full Ironman by the age of forty. At the time, I was the top salesperson in my field, having crushed my quota for several years. Upon returning to the mainland, Jack invited me to his sales workshop that was taking place in my town. Wow! The infectious energy that erupted from my mild-mannered friend was astonishing. I quickly saw that things that I did well could be so much better. I always had goals, but they were never in writing … nor were they as comprehensive and specific as they should be. Adopting Jack's principles has made a profound impact on my life over these past fifteen years, and I have shared them with employees and mentees to help them achieve their goals. My advice to readers of this book? Immerse yourself in the concepts, and take action."

—**Chris Jannuzzi**

"Rarely in life do you come across individuals who have followed an intentional path that has led to great happiness, accomplishment, and meaningful contribution. Even more rarely do you find those same people who can share how they accomplished that life. Jack has done this in his newest book that imparts a wisdom that, if followed, will make your life exceptional. This should be required reading for anyone at any age!"

—**Steve Kirstiuk,** Vice President APS-USA, Advantage Parts Solutions

"My first experience getting Jack'd was in 1994 at the YEO International University. Jack gave me the original idea that it is truly possible to live the life of your dreams.

Through Jack's many teachings, I have learned to dream big, then dream bigger and get busy getting it done. As a fan and friend of Jack Daly for the past twenty-seven years, I have watched Jack walk the walk. He is a man who sets the example for those of us that want to step up in our lives!"

—**Ron Miller,** Chairman of the Board, StartEngine

"I have known Jack for sixteen years, and by far, without a doubt, I have *never* met anyone who attacks life as does Jack Daly! It's not even close.

Sharing this now for the first time, there have been moments when I have been beat down with my businesses, recovering from surgeries, unable to walk, and there was Jack. No matter what always positive, inspiring, and forward looking with the strong dose of kick-ass that I needed … Jack Daly inspires me to do better in my life and in business every day!"

—**Paul Berman,** Serial Entrepreneur

"As Jack was walking away from my car, he turned and came back, stuck his head inside, and asked, 'Would you rather have twenty speaking gigs at one thousand dollars each or two at ten thousand dollars each? The money is the same, but two takes a lot less time. My advice is you tell the next twenty people who ask you to speak that your fee is ten thousand dollars, and if only two out of the next twenty say yes, you've made the same amount of money with a fraction of your time committed. As you grow, you can ask for more, but always protect your time.'

The man knows how to speak what he's thinking … The next couple of days Jack was a keynote speaker as well as led a full-day Get Jack'd workshop. He shared that Bonnie wasn't doing well, but she encouraged him to attend as she felt someone needed to hear what he had to say.

A year later, I texted Jack to let him know that his time away from his precious wife was not wasted. I had doubled my previous goal and sold over $86 thousand in recurring revenue, which had doubled what I had done in previous years and set us up for an additional million dollars the following year! Jack is nothing short of inspiring, and I cannot imagine where my mindset would be had I not picked up his book, had conversations, and attended his workshop. I am currently on my second week of a work vacation in Mexico with my wife, listening to the waves crash as I write this. Follow Jack to learn how to live the good life, grow your sales, grow your mind, and forever change the way you see your future!

Jack, I personally want to publicly thank you from the bottom of my heart for laughing and bursting my bubble that evening, as it was one of the best things that has ever happened to me and my mindset … Thank you, sir!"

—**Charles Henson,** Owner, www.NashvilleComputer.com

"If you're looking to enhance your life, let *Jack Daly's Life by Design* lead the way. Victory loves preparation, and Jack's book will give you all the positive energy and take on the world attitude you need to win over and over again. Woo woo!!! Bam!!!"

—**Randy Cohen,** Chief Energizing Officer, TicketCity and Z'tejas Restaurants; Author of *Secrets of Swagger*

"Hearing Jack speak at a conference years ago changed my life. I found myself wanting to be surrounded by him, asking him hundreds of questions, showing up to his seminars, and filling my notebook with his ideas. Jack transformed my viewpoints on life, professionally and personally. After reading this book, I can proudly say Jack is my Jim, and my success is a reflection of his commitment and heart to helping others grow."

—**Klyn Elsbury,** Keynote Speaker and Sales Strategist

"Jack Daly has become one of the best speakers and coaches for helping leaders be more successful, and many have wondered how he did that. The answer is simple, and it is the focus of Jack's new book, *Jack Daly's Life by Design.* Jack became a speaker and executive coach after a long career as a successful entrepreneur who lives an exciting life with passion and purpose. Jack does not rely on the theories of others to come up with the critical factors for success. He focuses on his real-life personal experiences to make his ideas come alive and be implemented. The rich examples he provides in this book make Jack an ideal role model that thousands of leaders now follow."

—**Mike Wien,** Six-time Ironman World Championship Finisher (two podium finishes); Two World Triathlon Champion Titles; Senior Marketing Officer for Frito-Lay, Pepsi, Omni Hotels, and Deloitte

"I have known Jack for eleven years. He has been an inspiration and positively influenced my life by design. When we first met, Jack encouraged me to get clear on what I was passionate about in the business, what I did not want to do, and have a vision of what the business would look like in future. Then backward plan how to get there. Ten years later we have ten times the business and have operations in New Zealand, Australia, the UK, Sweden, the USA, Mexico, and Singapore. I am living in flow and having fun. Jack also inspired me and held me accountable for running my first marathon. I went from a couch potato and not being able to run five kilometers to running my first of six marathons. This led me to completing five Half Ironmans and also one full Ironman. All of these extraordinary outcomes were direct results of Jack's living a life by design, not by default. Wishing you the extraordinary life you deserve."

—**Paul O'Donohue,** Founder and CEO, SalesStar.com

"If you learn best from honest and personalized stories, then this inspiring book is for you. I love Jack's insight about how to live life, and I love his energy, candor, and relevance. Actually, there's not much I don't love about Jack Daly. Treat yourself by reading Jack's latest book—likely his best yet. Go!"

—**Tom Londres,** CEO, Metro Commercial Real Estate (a national real estate services firm)

"'Jack Daly changed my life.' As a CEO coach and twenty-five-year Vistage member, and with twenty-five years in a mix of EO and YPO, I come across people around the world who blurt those words out when I mention that I know Jack. When I first met Jack, I was a small entrepreneur, my partners and I were doing around $2 million in revenue, and I was not that focused. My goal setting was average at best. Twenty-five years later the companies my partners and I own are over $100 million in revenue, and I have completed multiple Ironman races, achieved my black belt in TKD, and written eight books. Having Jack in my corner encouraging me to dial in my goals and live my life by design is a big reason for who I am today."

—Jason Reid, Co-CEO, National Services Group

"I'm blessed and grateful to call Jack a friend and positive influencer for over fifteen years. Jack is one of the great examples of one of my favorite sayings: 'Show me your friends, and I'll show you your future.' My future is brighter because I can count Jack as one of those friends. From triathlons, to participating in the Gathering of Titans program together, to speaking at our YPO events and consulting in several of my businesses, I've come to know and trust Jack's discipline, vision, and energy that he brings to any relationship or engagement. As I practice a *Life by Design* approach as well, I can attest that Jack lays out clear examples and a simple way to start your own life by design."

—Charles G. Hall IV, Chairman, Vitality Living

"So when I reflect on Jack and my relationship over the years, here are a couple of key words, phrases, and thoughts that I have:

1. Dedicated to excelling well beyond the normal scale of 1–10: the term *infinite* comes to mind.

2. A leader who, by his example, can motivate those he is in front of to do better than they ever imagined.

3. Has learned that the one thing in life that drives good orga-

nizations is leadership; he preaches this and lives his life that way.

4. The entrepreneur and the skill that these individuals bring to organizations can only be termed *priceless*. Jack's own career has been blessed by his work with these individuals.

5. Lastly, whether you meet him for the first time or, as in my case, for over forty years, you will walk away improved by the relationship.

Enjoy, as you read his book, Jack's learning and his 'big think' orientation. I know I will!"

—**Louis J. Gagliano**, Lifetime Friend and Learner; "At 76 the journey still continues!"

JACK DALY'S LIFE BY DESIGN

JACK DALY'S LIFE BY DESIGN

YOUR PATH TO AN EXCEPTIONAL LIFE

BY JACK DALY

Published by Advantage, Charleston, South Carolina.
Member of Advantage Media Group.

ADVANTAGE is a registered trademark, and the Advantage colophon is a trademark of Advantage Media Group, Inc.

Printed in the United States of America.

10 9 8 7 6 5 4 3 2 1

ISBN: 978-1-64225-308-5
LCCN: 2021918789

Cover design by David Taylor.
Layout design by Megan Elger.

This publication is designed to provide accurate and authoritative information in regard to the subject matter covered. It is sold with the understanding that the publisher is not engaged in rendering legal, accounting, or other professional services. If legal advice or other expert assistance is required, the services of a competent professional person should be sought.

Advantage Media Group is proud to be a part of the Tree Neutral® program. Tree Neutral offsets the number of trees consumed in the production and printing of this book by taking proactive steps such as planting trees in direct proportion to the number of trees used to print books. To learn more about Tree Neutral, please visit **www.treeneutral.com**.

Advantage Media Group is a publisher of business, self-improvement, and professional development books and online learning. We help entrepreneurs, business leaders, and professionals share their Stories, Passion, and Knowledge to help others Learn & Grow. Do you have a manuscript or book idea that you would like us to consider for publishing? Please visit **advantagefamily.com**.

To my life mentor Jim Pratt, who catapulted me to world travels and business wisdom, and to my "gone but never to be forgotten" wife, Bonnie, who shared so many of life's adventures with me. ♥

CONTENTS

PART 2: TIME TO DESIGN *YOUR* LIFE

PART 3: OBSTACLES & INSPIRATION

FOREWORD

By Rick Iovine

The importance of family and friends in our lives cannot be overemphasized. Many years ago, I hit the jackpot (no pun intended) when I met my lifelong best friend, Jack Daly. While we are not blood relatives, it would be easy for me to argue that we are closer than most "real" relatives.

Jack and I met at the ripe old age of five. As we lived through childhood and early adolescence, it was easy to recognize Jack had a plan, even at an early age. Life wasn't something to be taken for granted or left for someone else to design and implement for you.

We have shared an amazing number of life's adventures as we traveled through childhood, teen life, military service, adults with families, business associations, and life's memorable events. For the last thirty-five years we have experienced most of these things while living 2,500 miles apart. Who says long-distance friendships can't last or, even more importantly, continue to grow and remain strong?

Jack has impacted me in many ways and has always encouraged me to take a positive approach and action in whatever life deals you. He reminds me to focus on the importance of balance in life, and it has helped me be a better person, husband, and father. While I was always an active weekend warrior, Jack encouraged me to step up my game to get truly fit, and a little over twelve years ago, I completed my first marathon. I've completed several others since (only a fraction of the number Jack has accomplished).

We have been assets to each other, openly weighing in on important life and business issues. Friends like us don't keep tabs on who has more impact on the other, but if we did, I believe Jack would come out on the short end of the stick. I am extremely fortunate to have our friendship and to have shared so many life experiences, adventures, and accomplishments. We have many more to go, as Jack's bucket list continues to grow like a bottomless cup of coffee.

Get ready to experience a magnificent adventure!

Jack Daly's Life by Design will launch you into getting the most out of your own life. You will easily recognize Jack's energy and passion as he lives his message—in life and in business. As you read, you will ignite your own passions and realize it's never too late to design the life you want. Figure out what is important in your life, build your life's road map, and take actions to achieve your plans. Designing your life will enable you to live with confidence as you embrace your dreams and fulfill your purpose while imbibing the warmth of the sweet things in life.

Enjoy Jack's ride, and go out and design your own!!!

ABOUT THE AUTHOR

Jack Daly is a life adventurer, serial entrepreneur, CEO coach, keynote speaker, and business growth catalyst.

PERSONAL HIGHLIGHTS

- Married forty-seven years to his high school sweetheart, Bonnie, lost to cancer in 2017.

- Completed marathons in all fifty states and all seven continents, with ninety-seven in total and soon to be one hundred—scheduled for Athens, Greece.

- Successfully finished fifteen Ironman Triathlons covering eight countries and five continents and the World Championship, along with representing Team USA in 2012.

- Played golf at ninety-five of the Top 100 golf courses in the United States.

- Bungee jumped the world's first and largest bungee jumps and shark dived in South Africa.

NOTEWORTHY CAREER HIGHLIGHTS

- Jack relocated from the East Coast to Southern California and started a mortgage company with three colleagues. As CEO,

Jack led the company through robust growth in its initial eighteen months to 750 employees and twenty-two offices nationwide, and in its first three years, the company reported profits of $42 million.

- Working as a senior partner in a five-year-old privately held enterprise, Jack helped the company to be recognized as Entrepreneur of the Year by Ernst & Young and ranked number ten on the Inc. 500 list of the fastest-growing companies nationwide.

- World-renowned professional speaker specializing in sales, CEO coach, and celebrated author of several books garnering number one best-seller status on Amazon.

CREDENTIALS

- BS in accounting, MBA, Captain in the US Army.
- Vistage UK Overseas Speaker of the Year.
- TEC Australia Speaker of the Year.
- Spoken professionally on five continents, twenty-eight countries, forty-two US states, all eight states in Australia, and nine of the ten Canadian provinces, garnering top honors from his audiences numbering in the millions.

SUMMARY

An exceptional life.

Having built six start-up companies into national enterprises, I'm often asked to speak professionally to entrepreneurs and CEOs for my "lessons learned." One of the keys to success is to build a winning culture, where people who work in a company actually look forward to coming to work as compared to "having" to go to work. As Peter Drucker famously said, "Culture eats strategy for breakfast."

One of the pillars of such a winning culture is to offer professional- and personal-development opportunities. As you will read in this book, I have pursued a personal bucket list for several decades, and that pursuit has delivered immense happiness to me. Along my life journey I have ushered many employees to a similar pursuit—call it *pursuit of your dreams*, *bucket list*, or whatever. The feedback I've received has been most gratifying.

Imagine as a business leader having the bucket lists of those you lead and, each morning, waking up and reviewing such lists over breakfast, wondering whose dream you might help come true! Fact: I have several clients who are now doing this regularly.

Leaders, once you read this book, and if it resonates with you, please consider gifting it to each of your employees, encouraging them to reach for their personal stars!

Enjoy the book,
Jack Daly

ACKNOWLEDGEMENTS

What a treat to have my daughter, Melissa Daly Young, edit this manuscript. I handed her a very rough version of what you will be reading, and she turned it into a real page-turner. Once again, as she often has, she exceeded my expectations, and they were high to start with.

Once edited, I placed the rest of the book's journey into the capable hands of the Advantage publishing team. This is the fourth book that this team has produced for me, each time making the process seem smooth and easy. Thanks to founder and CEO Adam Witty for giving me the needed nudge to move forward with the books some ten years ago! Funny—I regularly forget you're the man behind the scenes, since I think of you more as a great friend than a business relationship.

So many people express astonishment at all I have accomplished in my life, particularly when reviewing my bucket list. Yes, it's a full life. However, so much of what's been done would not have happened without the creative and adept orchestration by my Business Manager, Jennifer Geiger. Imagine over two hundred thousand miles a year of world travel and juggling the business and the bucket list among all of that while ensuring I have a happy family life as well. Thanks, Jen, for all you do!

My friends span the globe, and so many have joined me in my journey that they are too many to individually mention. The lion's share of these friends came to me by way of a number of CEO mastermind organizations for which I have spoken. These groups facilitated my world travels and include Entrepreneurs' Organization (EO), Young Presidents Organization (YPO), and Vistage. Additionally, so many more doors to an exceptional life were opened by my speaking and coaching clients, and I want to thank them all.

As you will read in the book, two names will appear frequently: Rick Iovine and Mark Moses. These two guys have literally gone with me to the far ends of the world—Mark running marathons at the North and South Poles with me, and Rick joining me on the Great Wall of China and Machu Picchu and plenty of spots in between. Thanks for the memories!

Last but not least, big hugs go out to the love of my life, Karen Caplan. After losing Bonnie, my wife of forty-seven years, to pancreatic cancer, I had pretty much resolved to spending the remainder of my life alone. It wasn't a pleasant prospect but realistic. Then lo and behold, over dinner with my twenty-plus-year client Karen, we kissed. Since then, we have been inseparable as true life partners. Thanks, baby, for the push to get this book out into the world so others might benefit. I look forward to sharing life adventures going forward with you. Much love.

Success. To laugh often and much; to win the respect of intelligent people and affection of children; to earn the appreciation of honest critics and endure the betrayal of false friends; to appreciate beauty, to find the best in others; to leave the world a bit better, whether by a healthy child, a garden patch or a redeemed social condition; to know even one life has breathed easier because you have lived. This is to have succeeded.

—RALPH WALDO EMERSON

PART 1: MY LIFE BY DESIGN

People with goals succeed because
they know where they are going.

—EARL NIGHTINGALE

THE EARLY YEARS

People have regularly remarked about my disciplined, structured life, wondering where and how it all began. "Have you always been like this? What was the catalyst?" Another frequent inquiry is about how I amped up my game later in life. Fair questions. Here goes.

I was born in 1949, the oldest of five siblings. Our family would justifiably be classed as middle income at best. While my childhood mirrored others', I also recognized some early differences—beyond sports and general playing around, I found I enjoyed work, selling, and business.

My first job was more entrepreneurial than a "job." At six years old, I noticed that girls were making pot holders and selling them door to door to moms and grandmoms, similar to Girl Scouts selling cookies. Making the pot holders seemed simple, so I decided to do the same. When I knocked on doors, the moms told me they already had plenty, having bought from Mary, Sally, and Susie. I replied that they were all girls and they needed to have at least one, if not two, pot holders made by a little boy. Most laughed and bought! Looking back, I realize that the little girls shared the market, and I owned the market (as no other little boys made and sold pot holders). When you own the market, you can charge whatever you want, so I charged twice the price of the little girls. Now that was fun—even better than playing games with the other kids!

When I hit twelve years old, I went into the newspaper-delivery business. I took over a kid's route of thirty-two customers and a year later had grown the route to 275 customers. Between going to school during the day and doing mandatory homework immediately after, it was often dark by the time I could deliver the papers. Growing up in southern New Jersey meant it was often cold and inclement weather too. This paper-delivery job was simply not fun, but I did like the money. What I really enjoyed was the selling process. The newspaper company required carriers to be at least twelve years old, so I recruited five younger kids and split the route between them. The paper cost twenty-five cents a week for six days, and the company paid the carrier six cents a week. I split the six cents fifty-fifty with the kids. I then did all the collecting of the money and never agreed to split the tips, which was where the lion's share of the money was. So they did all the work, I was freed up to sell (which was what I enjoyed the most), and the majority of the money stayed with me. I sure enjoyed this "entrepreneur thing"!

Since I had my time freed up, I took the job of caddie at the local private country club. At first, I thought I knew what the job entailed—carry the clubs, find the ball, rake the traps, tend the pin, etc. My perspective changed dramatically after the first two weeks. You see, the members were playing golf on selected weekdays, along with weekends. They arrived in newer high-end cars, and they lived in fancy estate homes. Contrast that with my dad working every day of the week—no time for golf, a car with hundreds of thousands of miles on it, and a modest house. I sensed a significant opportunity. I suspect if I tried to get an appointment with any of the members to pick their brain on how they had achieved such success, at thirteen years old, I would not have gotten into their offices. But they came to *my* office—the golf course—and I had four hours to pepper them with my questions as to how they had achieved their success. When I reviewed the answers from what seemed like hundreds of members (likely closer to fifty members), there were several themes that surfaced: putting your goals in writing, developing a plan on how best to achieve the goals, tying in dates or indicators to measure accomplishment of the goals, and establishing some system of accountability to increase the probability of success.

Coming out of these conversations, I established four areas I wanted to achieve goals in by the time I was thirty years old: professional, financial, educational, and family. Once I established an end zone for each of these, I worked backward to determine what activities I needed to complete each year for each of the four goals.

My goals were:

Professional: be the CEO of a national firm in the money business.

Financial: be in the top 25 percent of income earners in America.

Educational: procure BS and MBA degrees.

Family: be married with children.

At thirteen years old, I figured if I could accomplish these, I would have achieved success by the age of thirty, and then I could work on my next set of goals.

> The future does not get better by hope;
> it gets better by plan, and to plan for the future
> we need goals.
> **—Jim Rohn**

This is a process I have been following ever since and continue to use to this day. In fact, you can find my one-year goals, bucket list, reports on activities, and narrative summary all posted on my website at www.jackdalysales.com. There are also some examples in the appendices of this book.

How did it work out? By the age of thirty-two, I was the CEO of a national financial services firm, and my annual income ranked in the top 10 percent of income earners in America. I earned my BS by age twenty-three and my MBA by age twenty-nine and was married at age twenty. By age thirty, I was the father of two children. Not bad.

My wife, Bonnie, and I married at the age of twenty and led a blissful life together as a married couple for forty-seven years. Sadly, she passed away at the age of sixty-seven, a victim of pancreatic cancer. One of the key ingredients of our magical life together came down to something I refer to as *terms of engagement*. I decided to have the tough conversations up front, as compared to so many who delay these conversations. From the age of thirteen, I had been pursuing my goals and living an intentional life. I knew things I enjoyed and things that I didn't—things I was good at, and things I wasn't. I helped Bonnie share similarly about herself. Better to know these things ahead of such an important event as a marriage. We agreed that we were attracted to each other for our differences as much as for our similarities. We promised to not change the other along the way. For the most part, we held to this, and I attribute much of our marital success to tackling big issues early. This is a life lesson that has done me well for decades.

By the time I hit my forties, I had enjoyed considerable success in my business career—involved at the leadership level of six companies, with employees numbering in the thousands. In my teens I had goals of being a successful CEO/entrepreneur and eventually exiting that career track to return to university life as a professor. That plan was to change in a major way after meeting my future life mentor Jim Pratt. Jim was a professional speaker hired to speak to our top sales performers in the company I led at the time. I intended to sit in for an hour or so of his eight-hour session with our sales performers; however, I was captivated by his teachings and stayed the balance of the day. This then led to hiring Jim as a speaker/teacher to share his wisdom with all twenty-two of our business centers throughout the United States. I decided to combine his visits with visits of my own, and we got to know each other quite well. I was so intrigued with Jim's life that I mentioned that I could someday see myself doing something similar. Jim asked me why, and I shared with him my lifelong ambition to someday return to a university, yet his life seemed so much more attractive, as well as significantly impactful to others. I highly valued what he was contributing to me, my employees, and our company. He certainly had made a significant positive difference in my life, both personally and professionally. He did the same for my employees, as he did with so many other companies. He and his wife, Nan, traveled the world, combining pleasure with business. And, as a bonus, the financial payoff far exceeded that of a university professor. He was leading an exciting life that I was envious of—traveling the world, making a difference, and generating attractive fees. Jim said if I ever decided to go for it, I should call him, and he would relish the opportunity to work together as partners. A few years later, at the age of forty-four, after accomplishing pretty much all that I wanted to in business, I did exactly that.

To say it was a life-changing decision would be an understatement. I went from a highly recognized, well-compensated business executive to the "starving speaker." The initial two to three years were comprised of long hours with little compensation. It would have been an easy reentry to the business world I had left, but the magnetic draw of the "life of Jim" fortified my commitment to see it out.

In fact, I recall vividly that I was the backup speaker for my first paid speaking gig, as the desired speaker had contracted the right to pull out within forty-eight hours of the event if they got a better offer. I got the call with two days' notice. The speech was an hour-and-a-half keynote on leadership and was the last of the two-day conference finishing at noon. In the first half hour as I spoke to a group of about six hundred, I had mental conversations with myself as to being the worst speaker ever. I needed to jump-start the delivery. Fifteen minutes later, I considered putting the mic down and declaring that I was ill. However, I didn't have the quit gene and kept going to the end. Once the gig was over, I quickly called the speaker bureau who had booked me and told them to call the client and apologize for my performance and state there would be no fee and that I would reimburse the speaker bureau for their fee. I seriously gave thought to retreating from this speaking career and returning to my more comfortable and familiar business-leader career.

Jim asked me several questions to get a feel for how that day had truly gone. He asked where the event had been held and the weather and the time slot. He asked what was to happen after my presentation. He asked how many attendees had left early. I answered that it had been on a Friday in La Jolla, California, with beautiful weather, ending at noon with a golf tourney and boxed lunches for the attendees. I estimated that maybe five or so had left my talk early. Jim then laughed and said I had done fine and I should not have the speaker bureau make the call I had suggested earlier, and I followed his advice. A month later I received a testimonial letter from the client indicating that I had exceeded all expectations. This is the only testimonial letter I have ever mounted on my office wall in the several decades I have now been speaking professionally. While I have received many such accolades since then, it is this first that holds such a special reminder that at times I can be my harshest critic—to stay committed, and success will be the reward. Thanks to Jim Pratt, I stayed the course and have enjoyed that life of Jim's that I so desired. Oh, the "secret" speaker that bailed, I learned later, was Bill Clinton when he was first running for the presidency, in the month of October! I'm sure glad I didn't know that before!

My role as a professional speaker provides me a platform to make a difference with people and companies, travel the world, and enjoy life. By this time, my children were well on their way to adulthood, and I no longer had responsibility for leading employees. This then positioned me to ratchet up more fun things on my bucket list and sign on for some challenging longer-term goals. Some of the newly added goals included running marathons around the world, playing the top golf courses in the world, and several more exciting adventures. As we look into my life by design a bit deeper, I'll share how these big items became my bucket list challenges.

As I look back on my life, I am filled with gratitude. I regularly pinch myself at all the incredible experiences I have enjoyed in my life. I recognize luck appears along the way in life, but I'm equally convinced that we can design the life we want and go about living it. That's not to say that life doesn't throw curveballs at you along the way. That's life, and we need to adjust accordingly. My intent is to share my journey in hopes that it inspires you to "up the stakes" in life. I hope to provide the reader a framework from which to accomplish what they desire. We have one life to live; why not live it in a big and exciting way? Let's go!

> I recognize luck appears along the way in life, but I'm equally convinced that we can design the life we want and go about living it.

19

LATE BLOOMERS

As I was writing this book, I wondered how many people would quickly dismiss it because they were "too old." Compare that mentality to that of Frank Lloyd Wright, who at age eighty-three, when asked which of his masterpieces was the best, replied, "My next one." You see, so much is about our mindset.

World-renowned Stanford University psychologist Carol Dweck, after decades of research, shows how success in school, work, sports, the arts, and almost every area of human endeavor can be dramatically influenced by how we think about our talent and abilities. In her best seller *Mindset*, Dr. Dweck finds that people with a fixed mindset, those who believe that abilities are fixed, are less likely to flourish than those with a growth mindset, those who believe that abilities can be developed.

I think of myself deciding to finally take on a triathlon, and at the Ironman level, at the age of fifty-eight, knowing my only swim stroke was a doggy paddle. Many would decide it couldn't be done. Yet with lessons and practice, within a year I was able to proclaim, "I am an Ironman!"

Do not let what you cannot do interfere
with what you can do.

—John Wooden

I found myself taking on these challenges later in life because from my early twenties to my forties, my life was one consumed with working, university and grad school, and being a husband and a father to two children. As I review my world travels and bucket list accomplishments, it's fair to say that most came well after these years. As we design our lives, priorities will change as the years pass. In those earlier years, my accomplishments were centered around loved ones and responsibilities to them. Once the kids grew up and ventured out on their own and I operated solo in my speaking business with no responsibilities to employees, I could more easily pursue my bucket list passions. Fortunately, my wife, Bonnie, was able to share in a considerable number of such events and encouraged me to pursue those that were out of her comfort zone.

> As we design our lives, priorities will change as the years pass.

So many people who have achieved great things have done so much later in life than we might expect. And so look at this list of famous people in a variety of fields who were able to go on and accomplish great things, regardless of their age.

- Ray Kroc: fifty-four—McDonalds

- Soichiro Honda: forty-two—Honda

- J. K. Rowling: thirty-two—*Harry Potter*

- Colonel Sanders: sixty-five—Kentucky Fried Chicken

- Grandma Moses: seventy-six—painter

- Julia Child: forty-nine—cookbook author / cooking-show host

- Taikichiro Mori: fifty-five—real estate investor (world's richest man at one time)

- Winston Churchill: sixty-two—prime minister

- Martha Stewart: forty-one—entertaining

- Rodney Dangerfield: forty-six—comedic actor

- Sam Walton: forty-four—Walmart

- Frank Lloyd Wright: eighty-three—was asked which of his masterpieces was the best and answered, "My next one."

- Willie Shoemaker: fifty-four—jockey who won the Kentucky Derby

- Jack Nicklaus: forty-six—won his sixth Masters Tournament

And so, are your best days behind you, or are they ahead of you?

"Ten years ago you asked the group of us at GOT (an entrepreneurial mastermind group) to reflect on the question, 'Do you believe your best days lie ahead of you or behind you?' At forty years old, I had a lot of good fortune come my way. In my deep gratitude for the life I lived to that point, I had this sinking realization in your question that I actually believed (and was living) like my best days were behind me. I had no idea I was coasting. It was a wake-up call for me. In that session, I stepped forward with the 'easy' challenge to the narrative I had, 'I could never do an Ironman,' following your own example of how you can. You were willing not only to inspire but to support, encourage, facilitate, etc. Six months later I completed my first Ironman, and at the finish line, to the call of "Tony Lillios, you are an Ironman," through the tears, I instantly began to wonder what else I had been convincing myself I couldn't do.

"Jack, you unlocked so many adventures for me. And those adventures led to a further opening of possibilities for me. I feel my growth anew in the last decade. I'm not sure I would have ever become a father had I not woken up by having you in my path. I am forever grateful for the impact you have made on me."

—**Tony**, lillios.com

The good news is each of us gets to decide! As my friend Paul Berman often says, "Turn your *what* into *when*!"

I could of course have retired and concentrated my energies on learning how to paint watercolors or how to beat my mum at golf. It wasn't and still isn't in my nature to do so. People asked me, "Why don't you have some fun now?" but they were missing the point. As far as I was concerned, this was fun. Fun is at the core of the way I like to do business, and it has been the key to everything I've done from the outset.

—**Richard Branson**

MY LIFE JOURNEY SO FAR

Most folks are so busy doing things they think they have to do that they never focus on what they actually want to do. And yet you don't have to take life as it comes to you. You design your life to be the way you want it to be—you can really turn *What if?* into *What is.*

"Someday … someday … someday …" We are all familiar with people expressing their wish lists this way. I met my wife, Bonnie, at the age of sixteen. Four years later, we married. As we were dating, we naturally discovered more and more about each other and our respective families. One of several things in common was each of our parents regularly having discussions about all the fun things they planned to do when they retired. Sadly, we each lost our dad by the age of fifty due to illness ending in too-early death. Those retirement days never arrived, nor did all those fun things they had planned. As such, Bonnie and I committed to "not wait" but seize life intentionally. This contributed to what we called *life by design*!

In John Anderson's *Replace Retirement*, he shares that "hitting your 'someday goals' takes effort. And it takes a plan. A written plan that can turn someday into reality."

I'm the type of person who sees his glass as bubbling over! Compare this with the pessimist who exudes negativity or passivity. Who do you think has the unfair advantage in life? As Dr. Dweck shared in *Mindset*, those with a growth mindset, who believe abilities can be developed, claim a distinct advantage in life compared with a fixed mindset.

Your journey is determined by the choices you make. Your answers are determined by the questions you ask. Your destination is determined by the steps you take. Your future is determined by what you do today.

Somebody should tell us, right at the start of our lives, that we are dying. Then we might live life to the limit, every minute of every day. Do it! I say. Whatever you want to do, do it now! There are only so many tomorrows.

—Michael Robbins

Witness the compelling story of my friend Shay Eskew, who chronicled his journey in his book, *What the Fire Ignited*. Here's a quick summary:

It's hard to believe two minutes in the life of an eight-year-old changed my entire life trajectory. On August 4, 1982, I, as well as my best friend, was accidentally set afire with gasoline by a neighbor's fifteen-year-old daughter. Luckily, I remembered to stop, drop, and roll, saving myself and eventually my friend. With over 65 percent of my body covered in scars, "normal" took on a whole new meaning. Once an attractive young boy, I now more closely resembled a horror-film villain. My face was disfigured. My neck was permanently stuck at a sixty-degree angle. My right ear was amputated due to gangrene. My right arm was physically melted to my side. It would take over three years to lift my arm over my head … had to write left handed to finish the third grade. The final blow was being told by doctors I'd never be competitive in sports again.

I looked around the ICU room and knew I didn't want to be a burn kid. I wanted to be an athlete. I stared at an autographed picture from Herschel Walker and committed to "living life intentionally" ... do whatever it took to mold myself into an athlete, no excuses, no complaining. I embraced my scars and decided to make the most of a bad situation. I knew I couldn't take away the scars, but I could change what I did with the scars. It didn't happen overnight.

Thirty-six years later, my body of work speaks for itself—inducted into the National Wrestling Hall of Fame (medal of courage), three-time College Boxing Champ, and five-time Ironman 70.3 AWA Gold Athlete (ranked top 1 percent worldwide). Most importantly, married seventeen years and father of five!

Life is messy. As you encounter the messiness in your life, the key is to decide how best to deal with it. Design your plans to reach your desired destination. Shay sure sets a high bar to inspire us all, and I thank him for our friendship.

Much of my life has been driven by my passion for business. Whether as an accountant, a CFO, an entrepreneur, a business executive, a CEO, a professional speaker, a trainer, or a coach, I've pursued each with energy and pure enjoyment. That said, I

> Life is messy. As you encounter the messiness in your life, the key is to decide how best to deal with it.

never desired to have my love of business rob me of the other joys of life. Health and fitness, family, finances, leisure, sport, spirituality, and personal growth and development were all areas I also wanted to prioritize.

It's my hope that sharing several of my life quests and accomplishments will be the impetus for you to pursue a "bigger life." Then assemble your written plan to make it happen, and take action!

THE VALUE OF TIME: SYSTEMS & LEVERAGE

The value of time was an early moment of clarity for me in life. Each of us is afforded the same 168 hours each week, yet some folks get so much more out of their 168 hours. While this 168 is mathematically correct (seven days x twenty-four hours a day), much of it is eaten up by obligatory activities. For example, if we sleep the doctor-recommended eight hours per day times seven days, we just lost fifty-six of those 168 hours. Add to that time to eat, exercise, be with family, and work, and you will quickly find that your 168 can disappear unless protected and managed like the treasure it is.

> If you don't make the time to work on creating the life that you want, you're going to spend a lot of time dealing with a life you don't want.
>
> **—Kevin Ngo**

John Anderson, author of *Replace Retirement*, puts this in great perspective: "If you reclaim just one hour of wasted time per day, it amounts to 365 bonus hours per year—the equivalent of nine forty-hour workweeks."

I've relied on two basic foundations in my life, employed both personally and professionally, which have enabled me to successfully navigate optimization of the 168.

These keys are:

Systems and Processes, and

Leverage

Let's look at each.

My first foundation is *systems and processes*. A simple example on the personal side of life is quite illuminating. I can vividly recall the many times in life when my wife, Bonnie, and I would make a dinner reservation, agreeing on the time. Fifteen minutes before we needed to leave, I'd inquire if Bonnie were close to ready, to which she would often reply, "Yes, I just need to find my keys." A hurried search for the keys would follow before we'd be ready to walk out the door. I set up a system—a rack upon entry to the house where we could put our keys. After implementing that system, we would never find ourselves looking for the misplaced item shortly before our scheduled departure. The reader could easily dismiss this as a small item to be citing; however, much of our 168 can be better managed and controlled by adherence to similar systems or processes. My friend Verne Harnish says it so well: "Routine will set you free."

The same is true in business. I have had the good fortune to build six companies into national businesses in the United States. These companies were fast growing, both on revenue and on profit lines. Company-wide systems and processes were key to their growth. As a business coach and professional speaker, one of my frequent mantras is "Sports teams are run better than most businesses." Key to their success is the playbook and the team's adherence to the processes in it.

My second foundation is *leverage*—how can I generate more in less time? A key component here is investing your time in the most important things. These are what I call HPAs, or high-payoff activities. Whether in my work with CEOs as a CEO coach or with salespeople as a sales coach, we consistently discover an extraordinarily high percentage of time is spent on things that are not what the individual expresses are most important. I find more than 50 percent of a salesperson's time is spent on non-HPAs. CEOs are also spending close to 50 percent on non-HPA activities. Unload some of these activities to others, and discover time to inject into the things we seek most in life! Another way to look at this is a quote I've often shared: "If you don't have an assistant, you are one."

> How can I generate more in less time? A key component here is investing your time in the most important things.

Here are some simple examples of this point. Going back to my twelve-year-old-newspaper-boy story, once I had built my route into 275 customers, I no longer had the time to sell more paper subscriptions, but additional subscriptions would increase my income. The selling activity was also where my fun was, my passion. It made more sense for me to hire kids in the neighborhood to deliver the papers as my "assistants" so I could invest my time in my passion and thereby generate more financial reward and fun.

Early in life, as a teenager, I realized that there were things I would like to avoid doing if I could: cooking, yard work, handyman work, shopping, and similar tasks only sounded like "work" to me. I committed to finding a way not to perform these life necessities— whether I had a partner or spouse who took care of them or had the financial means to outsource the services. By removing these from my 168 schedule, it allowed me to pursue the things I enjoyed most in life and accomplish more than the average person in a typical day, month, year, and lifetime.

My story as a thirteen-year-old caddie and the lesson on goal setting is key at this time. I sometimes ask my audiences who would like to be more successful than they are already. All the hands in the room always go up. However, if I leave the stage and ask any single person what *success* means to them, a lot of stammering is typical. You can't design your life without thinking about and deciding what you want your life to be. We must first determine what success looks like in order to map out the route to success. You can't get "there" if you don't know where "there" is. Since I was thirteen years old, I've referred to this as *backward thinking*: define success, and chart back to the present. Stephen Covey put it much more eloquently: "Begin with the end in mind."

It's how you organize your view of the future that determines what that future is. This visioning process, where you picture your life as accomplished, productive, and healthy, can truly enhance and drive your life. Here is what I drew as my future at thirteen to carry me to age thirty:

FINANCIAL	PROFESSIONAL
annual income	CEO
net worth	national size
top 25 percent	money business

EDUCATION	FAMILY
BS accounting	married
MBA	kids
lifelong learning	

There are innumerable examples where this vision I documented came into play, charting my life course. In high school, I was categorized as a college-prep student. My professional vision included being the CEO of a national company in the financial sector by the age of thirty. The beginning of my junior year, I was handed my schedule, which included chemistry and trig. I had already determined the best direction when I got to university would be to pursue an accounting degree (many of the adults I interviewed said it was critical for an entrepreneur/CEO to understand how the numbers worked). I felt business law and bookkeeping courses would have more value

> It's how you organize your view of the future that determines what that future is.

given my desired life direction. My father and I met with the principal and pleaded the case, upon which I was cleared to take the unconventional route of these business courses. This resulted in me getting a quick liftoff in university early on, so much of the material covered was a repeat from the business track I had pursued in high school. I'm convinced that none of this happens without taking the time and making the effort to dial in on your definition of success (your vision) and designing the route to that success.

As I look back over my life, it is amazing to see the number of accomplishments that happened because I wrote them down and shared them with others. I'm often told what an intentional life I've led. Most people marvel at this, while I have trouble thinking of living life any other way.

> By recording your dreams and goals on paper,
> you set in motion the process of becoming the
> person you most want to be. Put your future in
> good hands—your own.
>
> **—Mark Victor Hansen**

According to Dave Kohl, professor emeritus at Virginia Tech, people who regularly write down their goals earn nine times as much over their lifetimes as the people who don't. Eighty percent of Americans say they don't have goals, and 16 percent have them but don't write them down! So less than 4 percent write down their goals, and fewer than 1 percent review them on an ongoing basis.

Here's a taste of possibility. Recently, my year included travel to five continents, twenty-one countries, thirty-eight international cities, and twenty US states. One year! A few highlights include Jerusalem, the Holy City; Israel; a Kenya safari; a Mediterranean cruise; a marathon in Havana, Cuba; an active volcano in Indonesia; climbs of Masada and Koko Crater; and a Rim2Rim2Rim hike of the Grand Canyon. Hopefully, that whets your appetite!

MARATHONS

Some might look at my goals or bucket list and wonder if I've always had so many extensive, detailed, long-range goals. And so many athletic goals. Did I always run? Did I just decide to add marathons in every state when I started out making a bucket list? Should you throw in the towel or feel discouraged if your goals don't seem as big?

My goals and my bucket list have always been ambitious but not to the level they are now. I have been working this program for many years, and they have grown each year. Take running as an example. To look at my goals, you might think running and racing life have been a major life focus forever. Not true.

When I was thirty-six, my family and I moved to Southern California from the Washington, DC, area. Just before leaving for California, I started training for a 5K race in Georgetown, where my office was. The day of the race, it was cold and rainy, and I chose to sleep in. I figured I'd catch a race some other time. That "some other time" arrived a year later. An employee of our company told me the Heart Fund was running a charity 5K race that would start and finish at our office. Additionally, she said there was a CEO one-miler that day and that if I signed up for either (or both), she was convinced donations and participation would increase significantly. I hadn't done much running since leaving DC training for that 5K I had passed on, but the upside of increasing donations compelled me to say yes!

The memory of that early-morning one-miler is permanently burned into my memory. It was an out-and-back route, and I took off like it was a hundred-yard dash. As I tired, I asked a runner how far to the finish, and he said we weren't even halfway yet! The good news is I finished, with a high degree of humbleness. Then came the 5K. I didn't have to worry about throttling it back, as most of the distance was covered in a jog/walk.

When I made it back to my car to head home, several fliers for upcoming races were on the windshield. The more I thought about these races, the more appealing they became. I would train (how about that for a novel concept!), improve my finish times, raise some money for a good cause, and reap the benefits of better fitness and health. I was officially hooked! For the next couple of years, I ran one or two 5Ks per month, sometimes traveling sixty miles each way just to race a 5K. Looking back now, that's a head shaker, since the 5K is such a short race and typically over in thirty minutes! Unable to find many 5Ks close to home, I grew frustrated until I found some nearby 10Ks. I took the plunge and enjoyed that experience so much that it was a true rarity that I would race a 5K after that. For several years, my racing consisted of 10Ks, a ten-miler, and then half marathons. The more I raced (and trained), the better my finish times. Having successfully completed the ten-miler after justifying it was "just 3.8 miles more than a 10K," I employed a similar rationalization to step up to the half-marathon distance (13.1 miles).

During this time, I had decided to leave the comfort of the traditional business world in which I'd been participating the past twenty-plus years and enter the world of professional speaking. As discussed earlier, this was quite an adjustment, moving from the CEO position to the unknown speaker, with an income near zero as I started this new career path. With the uncertainty of the career future, my stress increased, and I sought some relief in running. Living in San Diego at the time sure made the running easy with great weather and coastal routes. My fitness just got better and better, and my finish times did as well. This running stuff sure was fun!

I vividly recall celebrating my first half marathon over a terrific home-cooked meal prepared by my number one cheerleader and wife, Bonnie, complemented with a great bottle of red wine. With the finisher medal on full display, and cheering with a wine toast, I started laughing uncontrollably. Bonnie wondered what was so funny, until I shared, "I just don't recall any time in my life when I celebrated doing half of anything." And with that I took a huge sip of wine. Bonnie looked at me and said something to the effect of "Are you serious? Do you mean you are going to take on a full marathon?" When I gave her that knowing wink and nod, she just shook her head as if she had been here before (just not in road races).

> If it seems like you have everything under control,
> you're just not going fast enough.
> **—Mario Andretti**

Well, I had just turned forty-five years old in February and decided to take on a full marathon. The whole idea was both exciting and daunting. Imagine my surprise when my wife, Bonnie, suggested we pick a race and both do it. What? Now by this time, I'd been running for eight years. Bonnie, never the athlete and having occasionally walked a 5K, was now proclaiming we would do a marathon together! In fact, she found a marathon that had a walker's division, which in her mind meant she wouldn't finish last, her great fear. That marathon was scheduled for October 2 in Portland, Oregon. That would give us most of the year to train. What a great idea; I was in!

With the races I had run in previous years, I had already been training, but for Bonnie this became an amazing, focused effort. Living in San Diego made the disciplined training a good bit easier, as each day seemed the perfect training day when it came to weather. Now with a marathon on the calendar, it was time for me to set a time goal and organize a structured run-training program. My goal was one that many first timers shoot for: sub four hours. Bonnie set her sights on six hours.

Race day arrived, and the weather was in the midfifties to sixties, ideal for racing. I felt well trained and ready for a big day. My first ten miles were right on schedule, but as I approached the halfway point, I noticed a blister issue. Never before had I encountered blisters on my runs, and this was truly painful. Realizing I had another thirteen miles to go, I continued to run while trying to avoid further aggravating the blister. At mile seventeen my right calf went into a major muscle cramp that stopped me dead in my tracks. As I bent down to try rubbing it out, the left calf seized up as well, and I toppled onto the street. A short time later a race med vehicle stopped with its flashing lights and offered to ride me in to the finish. I hadn't come this far and trained this hard to be taken in by the med folks. I told them I was fine and rubbed my calves until the cramps subsided. I struggled to get up but slowly began the long walk to the finish line. As my walk continued, my legs were able to resume a jog, then a slow run pace. The finish line was finally in sight, and I crossed it at 4:28:22. Success in that I finished my first marathon; disappointment in not achieving my sub four hours. After taking a rest near the finish line, I figured Bonnie would be close to her six-hour goal, so I headed out to the course to see if I could cheer her in. It was really special to see her cross that finish just under her desired six hours. Well done!

We headed back to the hotel for a late checkout, a shower and change, and a nearby late lunch of pasta. My feet were blister sore, and as we headed to the airport for the flight home, I decided walking in my socks was more comfortable than getting those running shoes back on! Bonnie seemed to be doing good physically, although she admitted that somewhere around mile sixteen, she'd thought it had taken her twice as long as her other miles, and she had felt lost and disoriented for a while out there. That night at home Bonnie declared, "I'm proud that I did it. I'm glad that I did it. And I have no idea why anyone would ever do that again!" Despite the pain of my blistered feet, there was no way I was leaving that sub-four-hour goal unachieved!

The next day I started researching upcoming marathons. Great news! I discovered a San Diego marathon was scheduled in a few months, on January 21. Right in our hometown! I immediately registered and resumed my training as soon as the blisters permitted. With cloud cover and midfifties temps, the stage was set, and I was ready. The good news is no blisters that day. However, I hit the proverbial wall at mile twenty-one. My legs felt like they didn't have five miles in them. I did the math and realized my sub four was still in play. To come this far and fall short would be heartbreaking. So despite the heaviness of the legs, I marshaled up any energy I had left and resumed my paced running. The finish line came into view, and the photographers were ready, so I picked up the final stretch pace and crossed the finish line in 3:58:58. My sub four hours was firmly in hand. I looked for anything nearby to sit down on and sat there collecting myself for a good thirty minutes. There would be great wine at dinner to toast that sub-four-hour accomplishment!

Over the next ten years, I would run eight more marathons, all in California. With the sub-four-hour monkey off my back, I decided to run them more to remain consistent with my exercise and less about finishing times. In fact, beginning with my third marathon in San Francisco, I brought along a camera and took photos along the way. This running just for the fun of being out there was a lot more enjoyable than running with the pressure to improve finish times.

In those first ten marathons, most of my finish times were around the five-hour mark, as I would stop for photos with people in funny costumes, with funny signs, or with cheerleaders. Photos of city landmarks were always fun to record as well. Several local marathons were run with good friend and coworker Rob Hill, who raced in the wheelchair division—talk about inspiring!

My sixth marathon was scheduled in San Diego, and I convinced several folks in our company to join me and take on their first marathon. While the camaraderie was certainly fun, race day was really hard for me, as I arrived pretty much untrained. My finish time of 5:56:44 barely beat that first and only marathon of Bonnie's, and I lay down at the finish line and proclaimed that would be my last marathon. Ha! Less than two months later, I was back in Los Angeles and posted a finish of 5:09:04 (amazing what a little training can do!).

The following year was my tenth marathon overall, and my fourth in Los Angeles was in March, and something would occur out on the course that would change my marathon direction for a good portion of the rest of my life. I was about midway through the race when a guy ran by me with a shirt that read "I've run a marathon in all fifty states." This sure caught my attention, so I picked up my pace and asked him about his journey. He said there was a club called the 50 States Club, and he suggested I give it a look. This kind of challenge fit nicely in my wheelhouse! Straightaway, I added it to my bucket list. So I'm ten marathons in, ten years, and "only" two states. That would sure change now.

I quickly went on to pick up four new states in the months of April, May, October, and November. With camera in hand, chronicling my journey, this was all about "checking the state boxes" and having fun. Charlottesville, Virginia, was my third state. Easy choice, as my daughter, Melissa, lived there and afforded us the opportunity for a visit. I remember my first fifteen miles were easy and relatively fast for me, but then Virginia rolled out the hills, and I finished in 5:04.

The following month found me in Coeur d'Alene, Idaho, for state number four. To add to the interest, I also had a bucket list goal to play the Top 100 Golf Courses in the United States, and this allowed me to add one of these courses to my list at the same time, when geographically logical. I now began coupling a top one hundred course with my state marathons to make for a packed weekend agenda. Just six weeks after Charlottesville, I finished this one a full nineteen minutes faster. Both the golf courses and the marathons were beautiful.

In the marathon sport, there is something known as the Big Six. The Big Six is completing the London, New York, Boston, Chicago, Berlin, and Tokyo marathons, and many runners have this on their bucket list. My fifth state (raced that October) was the Chicago Marathon, my first of the Big Six. It was also my thirteenth overall, and upon finishing it, I declared it was my favorite. Forty-eight thousand marathoners cheered on by one million–plus on the sidelines, and a flat track provides a great tour of the Windy City. I wrapped up that marathon-racing season on November 28 in Seattle, Washington. The four new states I picked up that year brought my state total to six and my overall marathon count to fourteen. I remember saying to myself, "Well, I'm on my way!"

The following February I turned fifty-six years old, and I sat back to assess the future direction of my life. I had completed a total of fourteen marathons covering six states. My work as a professional speaker had me flying worldwide, often one-hundred-thousand-plus air miles per year. My bucket list was ambitious. Taking the pulse as to whether what I was chewing on was reasonable and met the definition of *fun* was in order. I enjoyed the travel. I enjoyed the speaking business. I enjoyed the races. And I had several items on my bucket list that required travel, so the success of combining bucket list endeavors made all the sense in the world.

Pablo Picasso wisely said, "Our goal can only be reached through a vehicle of a plan, in which we must fervently believe, and upon which we must vigorously act. There is no other route to success." I asked my Business Manager, Jennifer, to consider the various bucket list items in the interest of combining several. This turned out to be an ideal approach, similar to our combining the golf and marathon in Coeur d'Alene. In fact, we decided to work to combine our speaking-gig travels with the top-one-hundred-golf-courses and fifty-state-marathon quests. For example, speak in a city on a Friday, play a golf course from the list on Saturday, and finish up the weekend with the marathon. Ah, the trifecta!

When you think about running a marathon in all fifty states, the question as to whether all the states have a marathon comes up. The answer is yes, and I suspect some are scheduled at the request of the 50 States Club! New Hampshire would be one of those questionable states, and the marathon in Bristol on October 1 sure reflected that. Bonnie and I turned that race into a beautiful long weekend enjoying the fall foliage in the northeast. I joined what looked like maybe two hundred marathon runners. The weather was perfect, and beauty was everywhere, including a few covered bridges to boot! When a race has such a small turnout, it spreads out pretty quickly. I felt like I was less in a race and more on a solo run in the country. No complaints; it was a terrific weekend.

Another example of combining goals—one year I ran in my birthplace, the City of Brotherly Love, Philly, on November 20. We used this race as a family reunion, with several relatives running races of various distances. My sister Valerie joined me in the full marathon, where I was reminded of her being a full fifteen years younger than me (another way of saying she handily beat my 5:15 finish). I'm sure I'm biased with Philly as my birthplace, but this race is one of my favorites. Starting at the base of the majestic art museum and Rocky Steps, weaving its way through the many sites of the founding of our nation, and coming together with a picturesque run along the river and through the park. It being a superflat course doesn't hurt!

State thirteen would go down in Little Rock, Arkansas, in March, a month after I turned fifty-six. At the time, this race touted its finisher medal as the biggest of any race, and it sure was. In fact, I suspect it still ranks as my largest. Weaving that bucket list goal into races also had me visiting the Clinton Presidential Library, as earlier I had added visiting the presidential libraries to my bucket list. This combo strategy was proving to be more and more fun and resulted in each quest being made just that much easier. My early decision of bringing a camera along on races was a real winner as well, and most of the marathons were coming in right around the five-hour mark. Sure, I'd lose fifteen to thirty minutes of time that could have been shaved off my finish times—but a small sacrifice given the capturing of a lifetime of memories!

Many find my goals ambitious and are astounded by how many marathons I complete in a year. Let me walk you through a couple more of my races and then demonstrate how it is all relative. One year on October 23, I lined up for the Marine Corps Marathon in DC. Fun to have my wife, Bonnie, and daughter, Melissa, there to run the 10K. Sister Valerie was unable to get into the race but joined me for miles six through about fifteen as a bandit, and she sure brings her smile and energy everywhere she goes. As a previous Captain in the US Army, I knew what to expect in terms of organization, and the marines certainly didn't disappoint. Starting at Arlington Cemetery was a moving experience. Having lived and worked in the DC area for seven years gave me all the more reason to look forward to this race. Finishing at the Iwo Jima Memorial and having the finisher medal draped around your neck by a marine, you can't help but get choked up and emotional. My finish time was an unimpressive 5:21, but the photos and memories were more than worth it! Yes, this state-race number sixteen went to the top of my marathon favorites. DC is obviously not a state, but my bucket list goal was the fifty states plus DC, so for purposes of counting the states, it was number sixteen.

One week after the Marine Corps Marathon, I was in New York City for my first NYC Marathon. The weather in early November can vary greatly, and as all runners need to make their way over to Staten Island by bus or ferry, the day starts very early. Once lined up, there is little to no shelter, and there are hours before your group is called to the start. This Sunday, November 5, had a low temperature of thirty-five degrees (that felt like zero), and the temperature never made it to fifty. It sure sounds like I'm complaining, but the emotion of the race and the start on Verrazzano Bridge, with a recording of *New York, New York* by Frank Sinatra blasting and over fifty thousand runners, is unmatched in marathoning. Once the two miles of the bridge are behind you, it's on to running through all five boroughs. Entering First Avenue at mile sixteen/seventeen, it's like there are a million spectators in size and sound. Truly deafening and a great shot of adrenaline to take you through the next ten miles. The race finishes up in Central Park, and when the day is done, some two million folks are out cheering you on. A pure *wow*! It seems as if runners from every country in the world are out there, and the mood is amped up and positive all day long. In fact, the race is beyond a day, as the city is race electric all week long. Just a week earlier, I had thought the marines had put on an amazing expo, but NYC was that and then some. Literally, people get lost in the expo! After snapping ninety photos during the race and being caught up in all the hoopla, I was blown away that my 5:12 finish time was a full nine minutes faster than the week before in DC. State number seventeen was now in the books and had zoomed to my favorite of all marathons.

I learned later that history of a sort was made that day. That was the day that the legendary Ultramarathon Man, Dean Karnazes, finished his legendary journey of fifty marathons in fifty states in fifty consecutive days. I thought I was a bit of a big deal having finished two marathons within a week. Well, Dean raced the Marine Corps Marathon the day I did but then went on to race in six more states before running in NYC. Lesson here is no matter how crazy or ambitious one seems, there's always someone out there taking it to another level. Moral of the story is go out and have *fun*!

I continued to work toward achieving my bucket list fifty states, usually completing several states a year, but some years I made choices that led to fewer state boxes checked. One such year, I picked up only two new states, despite finishing six marathons. This was a by-product of racing two more Ironmans; returning to the Boston Marathon, which I had loved the first time I'd run it; and turning one into a family event with the Goofy at Disney World. The Goofy was racing the half marathon on Saturday, followed by the full marathon on Sunday. When successful, you earn a finisher medal for each race plus an additional "Goofy" for doing both races that weekend. Over Thanksgiving the year prior, sister Marie had declared to the family that there was no way she would ever run a full marathon. I couldn't resist and challenged her on the spot that I was sure in the right circumstances she would. Again, she declared, "No way." I asked how much money it would take; she paused and said $3,000, to which I immediately responded, "You're on!"

She laughed. "What just happened?"

All declared, "It looks like you agreed to run a marathon." The rule was that she needed to meet the qualified finish time or no payment. From that point things got more interesting.

My longtime best friend, dating back to grade school, is Rick Iovine. I met Rick in kindergarten. We went to grade school together, high school together, and university together. We served in the ROTC and the US Army together and worked at the same company many times. Our families have shared vacations together, and Rick has joined me on several of my bucket list exploits. I could write a book on just our sharing life together, but let's leave it at we have been lifelong friends. Over the years I discovered that it's not the quantity of friends one has but rather the quality. This lesson has served me well as I have navigated my intentional life. Rick's two children are the same ages as my children. None of our "kids" had ever run a marathon, and they wanted to know how much I was willing to bet on them. This was beginning to look like a potentially expensive race for me, as we were now talking about young adults rather than middle-aged siblings! As it

> Over the years I discovered that it's not the quantity of friends one has but rather the quality.

turned out, Rick's kids—Rachel and David—both agreed to $1,500 apiece, and the game was on. My kids opted out, and younger son, Adam, laughed that the money was too low, and with the training involved, it likely would come to about twenty-five cents a mile! Once Marie got well into the preparation, she laughingly agreed.

Lots of "firsts" took place that race weekend. Rick completed his first half marathon, which I paced him step for step the day before the marathon. I was shocked when Bonnie opted in for the half and also successfully crossed the finish line (with minimal race preparation). Marie, Rachel, and David all were successful and collected their Benjamins. Sister Valerie and I joined Marie in her marathon journey, and we both claimed the Goofy! Lots of photos, lots of laughs, lots of sore muscles, and a lifetime of memories.

The following year presented more than the normal challenges in pursuit of the bucket list. Business opportunities were booming, and travel spiked. While this was certainly good news on the business front, it left little room for anything else. As such, only two marathons were recorded, both new states, bringing the total to twenty-six (halfway there!).

At sixty-three years old, I headed to Providence, Rhode Island, for a marathon only three weeks after two back-to-back Ironmans in a month's time (having added Ironman racing challenges to my bucket list). The weather couldn't have been better on May 1 for a race, and as I hit the halfway mark, I noted a time of 1:51. Remember, finish times for me no longer matter; it's more about checking the boxes and taking in the experience, capturing it all in photos. But heck, I rarely go sub two hours in a half marathon on its own! I felt really good, wondered what a BQ (Boston Qualifier) finish time for my age group would be, and suspected it would be somewhere near sub four hours. The one and only time I had finished sub four was my second-ever marathon at age forty-six with a 3:58. I decided to quit taking photos for the second half (sixteen had been captured in the first half), and I focused on maintaining my pace. Unlike most marathons where I run out of gas around miles eighteen through twenty, I continued to feel good and finished with my one and only Boston Qualifying 3:56. *Bam!* My twenty-eighth state marathon (Rhode Island) will always hold a special place in my running memories.

Talk about a travel year! Six weeks later I was in Anchorage, Alaska, to pick up state marathon number twenty-nine. I had spoken in Seattle just before the weekend and was returning to Seattle Monday to speak again, so it just made sense to shoot up to Alaska for the weekend race, as I felt it was "in the neighborhood." Blessed with another perfect-weather day for running, the first half was off to another good start, and I started to consider a new record. The second half of the course turned into rough trail and impeded my progress but felt good with a finish of 4:36. I took advantage of some extra time to explore Alaska and found it to be every bit as beautiful as I'd heard. Kinda "cool" to be out on the water and grab a finisher-medal photo with an up-close-and-personal glacier in the background.

As I finished up my thirtieth state (Minnesota), I realized that not only was I 60 percent of the way to the fifty states, but I had now run fifty marathons in total. At that point, I opened my bucket list and added *running one hundred marathons* to the list!

The year following, I was focused very much on my Ironman-related goal, and while I raced three Ironmans and seven overall marathons, when the year was over, I realized that I had picked up no new states, and without better focus, I would be stuck at 60 percent. Many of the thirty states completed were states with particular appeal to me or made easy by my other travels. The remaining twenty were going to require extra work to get them done! The following year I focused my effort and finished five marathons, all in new states.

A few years later, I was sixty-six years young and realized that I needed to step up the speed of tackling these marathons. I decided to put my triathlon actions on "permanent hold" and get laser focused on the marathons. By the end of the year, I would finish eleven in total, including six new states, bringing totals to seventy-nine marathons overall and forty-four states.

Along the way, I had added *a marathon on all seven continents* to my bucket list. In this quest, Antarctica is typically the big challenge. As one of my marathons at sixty-six, I took on a biggie—the White Continent Marathon in Antarctica. There are two options: flying in from Punta Arenas, Chile, or crossing the Drake Passage by sea. My good friend Mark Moses and I chose the flight option, figuring we would escape the often-angry seas. We were both surprised when Mark's thirteen-year-old son, Mason, opted in for his very first marathon. Adding to the excitement, we were joined by a group of runners logging a marathon on each of the seven continents in seven consecutive days, with Antarctica as the final leg. The flight to Antarctica is about a two-hour flight. The challenge is landing on a gravel strip with potential inclement weather. To the disappointment of all, but especially the 7-7-7 group, the plane was unable to take flight due to intense fog in Antarctica. This disappointment would go on for several days, until finally we got word of a window of clearance. By the time we landed and trekked to the course layout, the sun was setting, and we had to pitch tents for an overnight encampment. The pup tents housed two to three people, but don't use the word *comfortably!* Suffice to say, it was cold. An early-morning wakeup brought us to race time. The approximate six-mile route provided all racers the opportunity to see the others several times while out on the course. There was a lot less snow than expected, and once all racers finished up the run, we packed up and took the celebratory flight back to Chile. Not knowing how long it would be for me to return to the area, I said goodbye to Mark and Mason (school beckoned) and took in two days touring the beauty of Patagonia.

State number forty was Vermont. The Shires of Vermont Marathon was a few hundred runners on a weather-perfect day, routed through wooded countryside and legendary covered bridges. While quite a few folks refer to me as *crazy* with all my life exploits, I had to chuckle at the race start. The runner in front of me was wearing a bright-red-and-green shirt, and printed on the back was "1,400 Marathons—Larry." Now that's crazy! While I was in the area, I made a quick add-on the day before race day and visited the FDR Presidential Library in Hyde Park, New York—just another of my bucket list items: visiting the presidential libraries.

This same year, in my effort to add Colorado to my list of states, Bonnie and I arrived in Colorado Springs and invested two days in height acclimation while touring the Air Force Academy, US Olympic Center, Garden of the Gods, and Pikes Peak. All of this as I prepared for the marathon assault on Pikes Peak on August 16. Just five years earlier, I had taken this trek on, crossing the finish line just two minutes past the ten-hour mandatory finish time. When I had crossed that finish line the first time, they had presented me with a finisher shirt and medal, so I had thought that state was complete. However, as I had begun to assemble proof in anticipation of certification as a 50-Stater, the website had noted me as a DNF (did not finish). I suppose most would have just chosen an easier race than the 14,115-feet-above-sea-level Pikes Peak, but I viewed it as unfinished business. The race is a true trail run, with several miles being single lane with runners running down having the right of way over those running up. This, combined with thin air at the top, results in many slow miles. In fact, my last two miles getting to the top (halfway point of the marathon) averaged close to an hour each! The views were fantastic, the runners' attitudes were upbeat regardless of the thin air, and the weather was runner perfect. With about four miles to go to the finish, I knew it would be close to the ten-hour mark once again. Soon thereafter I tripped on a tree root and face-planted. I bounced back up as if on a trampoline, with runners just behind me remarking on my resilience. I reminded them we were close to the ten-hour max, and with bloody knees and elbows, I crossed the finish line in 9:45. Both of my Pikes Peak Marathons would prove to be my slowest finish times ever, and I'm so thankful to Jason and Justin Abernathy for planting the seed that I should take it on. (After all, they race the half on Saturday to the top and then the full on Sunday—as mentioned, there are always people out there crazier than you!)

My wife, Bonnie, also joined me for state number forty-nine at Crazy Horse Memorial in Black Hills, South Dakota. Mount Rushmore had always been on our bucket list, and this race provided us the opportunity to check that off the list. The race started at the still-under-construction Crazy Horse Memorial, which is right up there in size and grandeur as Mount Rushmore. Ideal weather on October 9, marking the final weekend before the city closed down in anticipation of the coming cold weather, and I was happy with my 5:30 finish.

When friend Mark Moses and I had shared the experience the prior year of running the marathon in Antarctica, we had been disappointed with the small amount of snow and limited route of the course. For sure, we had made the best of it and were glad we had made the journey, but we had gone in search of what we'd missed out on. We found that and more at the polar circle at the North Pole! Mark and I joined about two hundred other runners and ran through the endless ice and arctic tundra of Greenland, experiencing breathtaking polar landscapes in what turned out to be my all-time-favorite marathon. The race is a point-to-point race, ending at the airport, where the runners are lodged. The initial 10K is a loop on an ice sheet with snow to the knees. After completing that, it's a twenty-mile snow-packed route back to the airport. Temps were in the single digits, and winds were about ten to twenty miles per hour. Whatever we thought we'd missed in Antarctica, we got plenty of in Greenland! The race has a mandatory seven-hour time limit. After slogging through the first 10K, I had eaten up two hours and thirty minutes. From there I paced myself to finish within the allotted time, coming in at 6:42. Mark had finished about an hour earlier. We both agreed it was one of our favorite destination races, and we had traveled the world with several Ironman races as well. Since we figured our Greenland visit would likely be a "one and done," we opted for an add-on tour of Greenland. We participated in a bone-chilling dogsled outing and took in the Northern Lights. Most of the runners agreed that this was a race not to be missed—and not for the faint of heart!

I planned to complete my fifty-state journey with New Jersey as the last piece of the puzzle the year I turned sixty-eight. Having grown up in New Jersey from three to twenty years old, it seemed poetic to finish there. I registered for the October Atlantic City Marathon and anticipated plenty of friends and family living nearby attending. But before that race, Surf City, for my fifth time, awaited on Super Bowl morning on February 5. This race turned out to be extra special, as my son, Adam; his fiancée, Melissa; my sister Valerie; and her husband, Jim, all decided to join in on the fun. Valerie and Jim flew in from New Jersey, while Adam and Melissa came up to Orange County from San Diego. For decades I had been begging Adam to join me in a marathon, with no success. Little did I know that all it took was a fiancée who runs to get him in the race! Surf City proved to be their first. Melissa and Valerie crossed the finish together, followed later by Adam and me together, and Jim brought up the rear. It took Adam and I 6:07 to get the job done, but we were all smiles by the time of the Super Bowl later in the day.

Little did any of us realize that later in the month we were all to receive devastating family news. Bonnie, my wife of forty-seven years, was diagnosed with stage 4 pancreatic cancer. Our world essentially stopped with the news. Goals and plans were canceled, and all efforts were put toward her fight for survival. Two months after the diagnosis, which was unbeknownst to the Jimmy V organization battling cancer, I was asked to raise funds for them in conjunction with running the NYC Marathon. Given Bonnie's condition it was an easy decision to pass on this race; however, we both noticed the race date as November 5, the same exact date we had first met while in high school in 1965. We took it as a sign, and I agreed to participate.

As the year progressed, Bonnie continued her valiant fight, working her way through three different types of chemo treatments. As the fourth quarter arrived, it became clear that the New Jersey marathon would have to wait for another year. The NYC Marathon date was quickly approaching, just as Bonnie's days were clearly numbered. On November 1, I told her it was probably best that I skip the marathon on the fifth. She would have none of it. Literally hundreds of people had donated to the V Foundation on her behalf, raising a record-setting $220,296. Bonnie asked me to go to NYC and run on her behalf and said she would wait for me to return to California. The evening before the race, I was still wrestling with whether that was the right decision, but since the fifth was the fifty-second anniversary of the day we had met, if she were to pass while I raced, it would be somewhat poetic. My best friend Rick Iovine and my sister Valerie came out to cheer me on that rainy day. At the V Foundation dinner, the night before the race, I met Howie Kra, who had also raised a record-breaking amount of donations, and we are now great pals. Friends Mike Wien and Chris Jannuzzi raced as well. My buddy James Ashcroft volunteered to race step by step at my side, and at the apex of the Verrazzano Bridge, he captured a photo so good that the V Foundation uses it regularly in their fundraising efforts. It was a rain-filled day, and the emotions ran high all through the race. I'm thankful to all who donated in this fight against cancer and my friends who turned out that day to support me. The following day I flew home to California and rushed to Bonnie at the hospital. She beamed with joy that we were again back together. Five days later, on November 11, Bonnie passed away and will forever be missed by me and all whom she touched with her caring heart.

I completed my quest for fifty states the following year. I found a marathon on the coast of New Jersey on April 22: the Ocean Drive Marathon. On the way to the race, I made a stop in Boston to thank the members of a group of sixty entrepreneurs from around the world known as GOT (Gathering of Titans). Over a decade before, they had welcomed me to the group, and upon hearing of the V Foundation fundraising on Bonnie's behalf, they had raised more than half of that $220,296 by way of an auction among the members. It was truly a tearful reunion, and I'm forever grateful to them in so many ways. On to New Jersey from there, and I was once again surprised with all who turned out to either race or cheer the runners on. Too many to name individually, but a special shout-out to the New Jersey chapter of Entrepreneurs' Organization for supporting the day with commemorative T-shirts, food, and beverages—pure *wow*! The race was a relatively small race, enabling several of us to have podium finishes in our age groups, always an extra-special thrill. While the day was certainly joyous, it seemed strange to not have Bonnie there, as she had joined me in so many of the states, and we had shared that experience of our first marathon together twenty-four years earlier. Thanks again to all who joined me that special day.

A couple more bucket list checkoffs were in store for that year, including the completion of my quest for a marathon on all seven continents, and what better way than with the Great Wall Marathon in China? Once again, my friend Rick Iovine joined me for this amazing race and tour of Beijing in mid-May. Entire books have been written of the wonders of both Beijing and the Great Wall, and we found so much amazement on our visit. Cutting to the race itself, pure *bam*! The start of the race is about a three-hour bus ride outside of the city, so it began with a very early wakeup. The day before we visited the Great Wall to see what was in store for us. To say this would be a unique marathon layout sure is an understatement. Rick elected to race the half marathon, and we had the opportunity to line up together. The start was a three-mile jog uphill on roadway, and then the Great Wall began. Did someone say *hills* and *steps*? The section of the wall that was run was about three miles, and then the runners moved on to rolling hills winding through local villages. My camera sure was active that day, with so many iconic sights and people cheering us on. Once the runners hit the twenty-mile mark, it was back to the wall in the reverse direction from earlier in the day. I was pleasantly surprised through the first twenty miles, as I felt fit and had plenty of energy. Those feelings were soon to disappear, as the wall took its toll on me this second visit. There was an eight-hour cutoff for the race, and at the twenty-mile mark, that was clearly not a concern. Again, that was soon to change. Cold sweats, dizziness, an upset stomach, and leg cramps all hit me at mile twenty-one. I found myself crawling the steps four or five at a time, then sitting on the steps for a break. I began to question if I were in serious physical jeopardy. For the next two miles, the crawl seemed to be my major movement, resulting in both miles taking about an hour each! Now I had real concerns about the cutoff. The final mile on the wall, I somehow reclaimed my energy and legs, and now it was off the wall and onto those final three miles of roadway, primarily downhill. I proudly crossed the finish line in 7:47 and couldn't wait for that three-hour bus ride back to the hotel! The following night was a huge dinner celebration with the runners and guests, and Rick and I were beaming at the accomplishment and journey.

Upon my return to the United States, I was contacted by the V Foundation, asking me for a return run of the NYC Marathon. Given the record fundraising of the prior year—and the love story of my wife, Bonnie—the NYRR (New York Road Runners) wanted to recognize me as a celebrity runner. I returned that year, raising more money for Jimmy V, and learned what it's like to be treated as a celebrity on race week. Video productions, special transportation, pre-race food and heated tents, a feature on the big screen at Madison Square Garden, delivering symposiums, and a live appearance on TV as I ran the race were all part of the experience. Bonnie was with me in my thoughts all through the race. A great close to the racing year—ninety-three total lifetime marathons, all fifty states, and all seven continents. Next on the list was one hundred marathons. *Bam!*

I finished up that racing year with a marathon in Havana, Cuba, in early November. When I mentioned the race and a couple of days being a tourist for my first Cuba visit, my friend Howie Kra jumped at the opportunity. My longtime good friend Susan Leger Ferraro graciously opened up her condo apartment suite in the heart of Havana, complete with a driver and island tour guide. The Cuban people were welcoming, and the vintage cars and cigar factories were just some of the unique attractions. The course started and finished in the city center and was a 13.1-mile tour of the city, run twice. The rains came in for the second lap, and I crossed the finish line a few minutes before

Howie at 5:55. This race brought my total to ninety-five overall, and I identified my final five marathons to hit my target of one hundred the next year, with the final race to be in Athens, Greece. Little did I know that my race schedule would be wiped out when the next month, I slipped on one step in the house, fell to the floor, and severed my quad tendon. As such, the journey to one hundred had to be postponed until after recovery from surgery.

TRIATHLONS

Somewhere along my marathon journey, I started mentioning the Ironman. Where did that come from? At fifty-eight years old, I raced my first Ironman Triathlon at Lake Sherborne in the United Kingdom. I had added *racing an Ironman* to my bucket list twenty-five years earlier as I watched (on TV) Julie Moss crawling over the finish line in the Ironman World Championship in Kona, Hawaii. It's well worth taking a few minutes to watch her finish—the YouTube link is https://youtu.be/v3GjOedMd1M. I still vividly remember remarking, "My God, it is amazing what a human being is capable of doing as long as a person is committed to doing something." After all, the Ironman consists of a deepwater swim of 2.4 miles, followed by a 112-mile bike race, followed by a 26.2-mile run, all within time frames for each leg and an overall time. Julie was leading the race up until the last few hundred yards, and her legs gave out. She fell twice and eventually crawled her way to the finish in second place. After a couple of days of not being able to get that image out of my mind, I said, "I wonder if I could ever do something like that?" Within a week that thought had transitioned to "Someday I'm going to race an Ironman"—and an addition to my bucket list.

John Anderson, in his book *Replace Retirement*, says it so well: "Taking appropriate risks will look different for each of us. We don't need to be unwise or foolish just to prove something. On the other hand, we should never be afraid to learn a new skill or stick our necks out for what we believe." When I added the Ironman to my bucket list, I was thirty-three years old, married, and father to a three-year-old and a ten-year-old, in addition to being the CEO of a national company. I hadn't run a road race, I didn't swim, and I biked only recreationally with my family. Training and investing time in pursuit of the Ironman just then were not going to happen. I couldn't see missing out on raising a young family, neglecting my wife, and skimping on leading my company while asking the employees to give me all they had. But I could put it on the list for a later time in life when the kids would be somewhat on their own and I would possibly be in a different place in business. By then, the only person I would be asking to sacrifice and be tolerant with my training would be my wife, and Bonnie was always there to support me. Ironman participation is a terrific endeavor, and I have championed many people into the sport, but the reality is it is also a selfish sport, given the amount of training necessary to compete.

It was four years after adding Ironman to the list that I began running road races, starting with that first 5K. My first marathon was eight years later. Eighteen years after my 5K, an employee of mine suggested I try a triathlon. Jennifer Pfeiffer was a seasoned triathlete and convinced my business partner Mark Moses and me to take on a local sprint triathlon in Temecula, California. I dismissed her quickly, since at the time I didn't know how to swim! Jen said the sprint was really short, beginning with a 5K run, then a sixteen-mile bike, and finishing with a 150-yard swim in the pool. With my marathon background, I figured I could muscle my way through the run/bike, but the swim was still intimidating. You see, I could float and do a bit of a doggy paddle, but I still wasn't sure of such a swim after racing the other two legs. Jen laughed and said it was a six-lap pool swim and I could stand in any part of the pool. With that, I was in!

So here's this fifty-five-year-old guy, with butterflies evidencing excitement/anxiety, lined up with hundreds. My finish time came in at 1:31:47. On one hand, nothing to cheer about—on the other hand, plenty to cheer about. Mark, Jen, and I were all smiles at the end, and all the racers enthusiastically applauded Jen on her age-group victory. Over the next year, Mark and I continued to talk about the exhilaration of completing that triathlon and subsequently signed up for a Half Ironman on the Big Island of Hawaii to be raced in June of 2005.

Seriously, what was I thinking? The plain truth is I wasn't thinking. This race was comprised of a 1.2-mile deepwater swim in the ocean; followed by a fifty-six-mile bike race in the hills, heat, and winds of the Big Island; and then capped off with a 13.1-mile run at the height of the heat and humidity. I arrived having "raced" just one previous triathlon, that pool swim sprint. I needed to rent a bike on the island, with no idea of how to switch the gears, and had to have the bike outfitted such that I could pedal with my running shoes, as I had never used bike shoes. And I had yet to take a swim lesson! Add to this the absence of any concept of nutrition while out racing, and racing in my running shorts and a T-shirt! For a guy who is generally known for his planning and systems and processes, this race could have been appropriately titled "Jack's Folly."

The swim start had more than one thousand competitors all jammed together, treading water, awaiting the gun start. I've often heard the gun start is like turning on a washing machine, and it was that and then some. Within the first one hundred yards, I had been literally swum over by several athletes, been punched in the head and other body areas as the swimmers reached out with their swim strokes, and had my goggles ripped off more than once. I found myself hyperventilating and decided to pull up and let the masses go by me. After composing myself, I set sights on the first directional buoy. Bonnie said it was easy to single me out among all the others, as I was the only one never putting their head into the water as I doggy-paddled into the deeper and deeper waters. Boy, that first marker sure was a long way out there! When I made the turn and headed for the next marker, now swimming parallel with the beach, I noticed a friendly guy easily lying down on a surfboard and keeping pace with me. Since I had raced so many marathons previously, I was well acquainted with what's known as the *sweeper* and asked this fellow if that's what he was. He acknowledged that there were a few of us out there who were significantly behind the masses, and they were there for our safety. He encouraged me to keep going, as I wasn't yet last and there was still a chance I could finish under the allotted time of one hour and ten minutes. He also served as somewhat of a directional beacon, enabling me to maintain a somewhat on-course direction. As I approached the coast, there were several of his colleagues cheering me on from the water, telling me I was really close to making the cutoff. Now, at this particular race, you need to climb up the coastal beach and cross the timing mat to be official and allowed to continue on to the bike. I was green-lighted to do that and, later in the day, would discover that my swim time was 1:02:51. I was happy to have made it, despite feeling a good bit beat up. Never had I swum so far.

It took me several minutes to get to the bike area, and most all the bikes were gone. I hopped on my bike, and off I went. That fifty-six-mile bike ride sure wasn't easy, especially the six-mile climb to Hawi, the turnaround point. Good news was that the return offered a good bit of downhill, although the final twenty miles or so was into headwinds. I entered transition two with a bike time of 3:51:58 and was told I had once again made the cutoff. All that was left to do was the 13.1-mile run! Well, that was what I was telling myself, but that "all that was left" comment sure was off the mark. You see, I had never before expended four hours of intense cardio work before a 13.1-mile run. And by that time, the heat and humidity were up considerably. That 13.1-mile run took me 3:05:11, and I gratefully crossed the finish line in 8:11:00, at which time I couldn't wait to just sit down. When I tried to sit on the grass, I found I couldn't bend all the way down, so I crouched down and let gravity bring me to rest. Upon hitting the ground, my entire body went into cramps. The medical crew rushed over, put me on a stretcher, and took me to the med tent for a total-body ice down. While all that was going on, the awards festivities were taking place. My buddy Mark Moses went over to take it all in, and I discovered later that I had won an award—the last person to exit the water on time and finish the entire race. Mark approached the stage to claim my award and was presented with flippers, water wings, and a snorkel. He made sure to let all know he was picking it up for his pal recovering in the med tent. Bonnie; Mark; Mark's wife, Ivette; and I spent the rest of the week taking in the relaxation Hawaii always offers.

The following year my business understudy Gerry Layo let me know he had signed up for the sprint triathlon in Temecula, so I decided to join him in a repeat of that initial triathlon race two years prior. I was still doggy-paddling in the swim, and I was even slower than before for the 150 yards. My overall finish came in at 1:31, exactly what I had posted two years previously. Three weeks later I took on an international distance triathlon in Palm Springs, finishing in 2:33:54. I used this race as a warm-up, as I had decided to return to the Big Island and take on the Honu Half Ironman in June. Still without swim lessons and training, I wanted to see if I could better my year-earlier performance. On race day, the sea was unusually rough. Once again, I was solidly in the back of the pack but exited the water with everyone congratulating me on making the cutoff. I stopped for a minute to hug Bonnie and head off to the bike. However, when I crossed the beach area and got to the timing mat, I was informed that I had missed the cutoff. What a rookie mistake! I had forgotten the key was to get to the timing mat. As such, I was not permitted to continue with the bike and run. I was crushed. Bonnie and I spent the day cheering our friends on, but I committed to that never happening again, as I was going to return to the mainland and get both swim lessons and practice.

Mark Moses introduced me to his swim coach, Steve Eisenhauer, and from there it was game on. I looked for another race to shoot for and found a 70.3 Ironman in Napa Valley in late July. This would give me nearly two months of lessons and practice, and I readily signed up. Since Bonnie and I were serious Napa and wine fans, a long weekend visit sounded perfect. The swim was in a river and was a wave start. I was superexcited, and when the gun went off, I found myself with serious breathing issues. For one hundred yards, I kept trying but couldn't get the issue under control. I literally thought I might be having a heart attack and pulled myself out of the race. That made for two DNFs (did not finish) in a row, and I was truly bummed out. I decided to take a ride on the bike back to the hotel, where I met Bonnie, and we spent the day wine tasting. While that has always been an enjoyable outing for us, this particular day was not so much so.

The time had now arrived for me to make a big decision. Should I pack this triathlon thing in and return to my enjoyable marathoning or step up and make a full commitment to the triathlon sport? By now I had invested in a high-quality triathlon bike, a wet suit, and the many other small peripherals associated with the sport. What gnawed at me the most was that bucket list entry twenty-four years earlier to race a full Ironman. So I went back to my swim coach, Steve, and asked how confident he was about my ability to tackle the full Ironman. He said 100 percent, and that was all I needed. Let's go!

> If you acknowledge that your dreams and hopes are worth working for and focus your thoughts on achieving them, your chances of empowering your life will exponentially increase.
>
> **—Ari Kiev**

Eight months later I was scheduled to be in Australia for business, and Mark Betts, an Aussie friend, suggested we race the Mooloolaba International Triathlon. So here I was with plenty of practice and lessons with swimming, hundreds of miles of biking, and my typical running, excited to be ready to take it on. Every one of the three legs of the race ended up slower than the Palm Springs International a year earlier—what a buzzkill. I crossed the finish in 3:01:40, compared with Palm Springs at 2:33:54. Here I was at fifty-eight years old, competing in the triathlon sport yet feeling deflated with my declining performance. I returned to the United States and seriously amped up my training workouts.

After this amped-up training, I was back for round three at the Honu 70.3 Ironman. I felt fit and well prepared. I had learned plenty over my triathlon journey. I exited the water as a "middle of the packer" with a time of 43:03 and was truly elated. Even better, I exited the water with an incredible amount of energy. Those swim lessons and practice swims were finally paying a dividend. The bike course is always a challenging one in Honu, as it's essentially half of the World Championship's full Ironman course. I finished the bike in 3:11:00, a very solid time for me. I hit the run feeling strong for the first 10K and then ran out of gas, finishing at 2:26:00 for an overall finish of 6:28:55—however, beating my two-years-earlier finish by one hour and forty-two minutes. Better still, I won a spot in that year's 70.3 Ironman World Championship to be raced in Clearwater, Florida. To say the least, it was a definite week of celebration on the Big Island!

I came home charged up and decided it was time to move up to the challenging 140.6 Ironman. I started to make a list of the possible full Ironman races that I could entertain for the next year and check that twenty-five-year-old box on my bucket list. As I was making the list, Ironman UK popped up as an August race. It dawned on me that I was actually going to be speaking in Ireland in August and London shortly after, and of all things, the Ironman fell squarely in between those gigs. Now, mind you, I had been thinking about the following year, as I was still learning the swim mechanics and much training would be needed to double the race length. I bounced racing it in two months off swim coach Steve, and he laughed and said, "You aren't really ready for a full yet." At the end of our swim lesson, he followed it up with, "Heck, since you are going to be over there anyway, why not? Even if you DNF, it will be a good learning experience." That's all I needed, and I immediately registered for Ironman UK, just two months away.

A month after Honu, I headed up to Napa Valley for some "unfinished business" in the Vineman 70.3 race. I struggled with that river swim again but was committed to getting it done, coming out of the water in a less-than-stellar one hour, but I made it. Both the bike and run were a struggle, and my overall finish came in at 7:19:44. We enjoyed all that the wine country of Napa offers and then headed home to Southern California. Clearly the Ironman next month was going to be a huge effort, but I was resolved to treat it all as a learning experience.

This visit to the United Kingdom in August was to be Bonnie's and my first time in Ireland and London. We contacted our lifelong best friends Rick and Kathy Iovine, and the four of us decided to visit London for a few days and Ireland for several more days. The vacation couldn't have been better, and we were blessed with fantastic weather. If you can imagine an activity in either London or Ireland, we did it! The Iovines then returned to the United States, and Bonnie and I went on to Northern Ireland for my speaking gigs. Immediately after, we were on our way to the United Kingdom and Lake Sherborne in Dorset. The weather sure took a turn for the worse, and the rains seemed unrelenting.

Race day arrived, August 19, and while it was partly cloudy, the rain had at least stopped. Bonnie asked when I expected to come out of the swim so she could greet me upon leaving the lake. I laughed and told her I had two hours and twenty minutes to get it done, and as long as I did that, I would be happy. When she pressed me for a bit more clarity, I said it would be at least one hour and thirty minutes but more than likely one hour and forty-five minutes to two hours. The course required two laps around the lake, and as I was making the turn for lap two, I noticed the lead swimmers headed to shore. *Head down and keep going* was all I could think. Finally, I arrived at the swim exit, and volunteers were there to assist the athletes out and strip us of our wet suits. As I headed to the bikes, I glanced down to check my time, and man, was I disappointed—my watch must have gotten bumped somewhere out in the swim and had stopped at 1:22:39. Oh well—I'd made the cutoff, and I'd be biking without a clock. When I started the bike, I looked down at my watch and noticed it actually hadn't stopped but was running all along. That meant I had just finished a 2.4-mile swim in under an hour and a half! That sure was progress from my earlier doggy paddles and gave me extra momentum for the bike.

Back at the lake, poor Bonnie showed up at 1:25, just missing my grand exit. She waited for every athlete to finish and eventually asked the race official if all athletes had been accounted for and was told yes. With that she phoned our daughter, Melissa, back in the United States and asked her to look up when I had come out of the water. Melissa informed her of the good news. Bonnie said she could just imagine how excited I must have been upon exit!

The bike was three loops in the rolling countryside, with one particularly long steep climb. After scaling that hill the second time, I suffered a flat tire. Ugh! In an Ironman race, you cannot accept any outside assistance or you suffer an immediate DQ (disqualified). The challenge here was that I had never changed a tire! I had all the necessary items and went to work. I really struggled, and it was painful to watch the many competitors riding by me. Finally, the tire was fixed (tire soft but serviceable), and I limped into the bike finish in 7:38:59. The combined swim and bike must be completed in under ten hours, which meant I had a full hour cushion on the allotted time. With a seventeen-hour total max time allotted for completion, this translated into me having nearly eight hours to complete the marathon. While I was in a race zone I had never before experienced (nine hours of max-out cardio already expended), I felt fairly confident that I could beat the seventeen hours and would check that bucket list goal later in the day. This made for a pretty pleasant run, as I could taste the sweet success!

At mile sixteen I found myself in a cold sweat, with weakness in my legs and a bit of the shakes. I reached a race table with snacks and fluids and asked if I could take a seat on the table. After sitting down for about ten to fifteen minutes (felt like an hour as I watched other competitors pass me by), I felt the sweats disappear and realized I had not done a good job at replenishment and nutrition. I picked up the pace and finished the 26.2-mile run in 5:33:38 for my first Ironman finish in 14:51:18. As I crossed the finish line, I heard it loud and clear: "Jack Daly, *you* are an Ironman!"

I was hooked, and I knew it. Three weeks later I raced an Olympic-distance tri in Los Angeles; then in November it was on to Clearwater for the 70.3 Ironman World Championship. I had a "solid for me" swim at forty-three minutes and a best-ever bike of fifty-six miles at 2:55; my pacing was absent, and the run ended up more of a walk, coming in at 2:25. I crossed the finish line both physically and emotionally spent with a best-ever 6:14 finish. Truth be known, I couldn't buy enough stuff in the logo-wear tent. In fact, it necessitated buying a new suitcase to bring it all home.

Over the next eight years, I was all about triathlons while also racing my marathons worldwide concurrently. I put a couple more entries onto my bucket list. The first was to qualify and finish the Ironman World Championship in Kona, Hawaii, and I completed that five years later. Racing an Ironman on all the continents (except for Antarctica, which obviously doesn't host one) was also added to the list. Three years later, that was completed with Ironman South Africa in Port Elizabeth, garnering me a podium finish with a third-place age-group finish at a time of 13:19. Over a twelve-year period, I would race fifty-eight triathlons. They broke down into three sprints, twenty Olympics, seventeen Half Ironmans, fifteen full Ironmans, and three DNFs. What a great and joyful journey!

My full race history is in the appendices for those interested, but here are a few more highlights that drove my momentum.

I raced the San Diego International and broke my distance times in all three legs, resulting in a 2:18 finish. Not only did I win my age group, but I was also named as the oldest finisher in the race, at fifty-nine years old. As the crowd cheered me on at the awards festivities, several thoughts passed through my mind:

1. the original Honu half, where I missed the festivities as I was iced down in the med tent,

2. a genuine feeling of pride with my first-place accomplishment, and

3. how did I (at just fifty-nine years old) end up being the oldest finisher?

Several triathlons and Ironmans later, I raced the Frogman 70.3 in San Diego. This race had become quite legendary given its location adjacent to the Navy SEAL school in Coronado. Having served in the US Army as a Captain, I was always an admirer of the SEALs. I had read several books about the SEALs and couldn't imagine in my youth ever placing my helmet on the deck and ringing the bell to indicate I had quit the opportunity to be a SEAL. Yet, historically, 80 percent of the candidates did just that. The swim start was in three waves, with the older competitors in the third wave. The course was two loops. After the first loop, you had to run the beach a stretch and reenter the ocean swim. When the first wave went in, the ocean was like a sheet of glass. By the time the third wave was ready to start, the ocean's waves had kicked up considerably. The swimmers would get near to clearing the wave crest, and bam, they would be dragged along the ocean floor back to the shoreline. I watched as swimmer after swimmer raised their hands to have a Sea-Doo take them back to shore for a DNF. As I kept fighting to clear the breakers, I had a conversation with myself, saying that I had just completed a 70.3 race in Honu two weeks prior, so who needed this aggravation? As I was getting ready to signal "no more" for my Sea-Doo ride to safety, I realized that I was about to "ring the bell" and quit! Right then, there was no way.

I fought as hard as I could and crested the wave. The remainder of the swim on the first lap was pretty smooth sailing, and as I swam to shore, I realized I needed to go back out and do it again. However, this time I knew I could do it, and somehow the waves weren't the obstacle they had been on the first lap. I was happy to climb out of the water in an hour and four minutes. The bike race was flat, and despite some headwinds, I finished that leg in three hours and ten minutes.

Half of the 13.1-mile run was in the beach sand, a scene I'd often played out in my SEAL reading. The sun was hot, and I was truly spent. I crossed the finish line in just under seven hours and wanted only to get in the car and ride home for the hour-plus ride. Bonnie hugged me at the finish line and said the finisher shirts were just up around the bend. I told her "Who cares—I just want to go home," and that was exactly what we did. Later that week I was on the road for a couple of speaking gigs, and Bonnie asked if I had checked out the website of the race. I said, "Hell no! Why would I do that? That race was brutal." She then informed me that I had garnered a second-place finish in my age group. I was elated, and then she mentioned not to get too excited, as there had been only two finishers in my age group. I slept well that night knowing there had been ten in our age group that morning, but eight had "rung the bell."

Seven weeks later I was in Florianópolis, Brazil, for another Ironman. I was registered in a select group racing in Ironman XC (Executive Challenge), which had a smaller field of competitors, increasing your chance of winning a coveted slot in the World Championship (now a bucket list item for me). That day I was at my best and recorded a lifetime-best finish at 13:10:55. Alas, only good for second place in my age group, when I needed a first! As added bonuses, I had six good friends who competed that day, and Bonnie and I snuck in a great vacation in Rio de Janeiro. The hang glide in Rio was spectacular and knocked off yet another item on my bucket list. What a life!

A month later I returned to my birthplace, Philadelphia, for an Olympic tri. My sister Valerie had now gotten a taste of triathlons, and we each felt we could beat the other. Several bets were made, and we both arrived with a gallery of friends and family to witness the battle. That morning we learned that in the sprint race the day before, a competitor had gone missing, and the feeling was that he'd likely drowned. As such, our race was turned into a 5K run, a twenty-five-mile bike, and a 10K-run finish. Immediately, all bets were off! Valerie is an accomplished runner and fifteen years my junior, so the race tilted in her favor in a big way. We started together in the run, and she quickly left me in her dust. Realizing I was stronger on the bike, I was intent on reeling her in on the bike and hoped to hold her off on the run. As the miles passed by, it was more and more clear that she was giving it all she had. With about four miles to go, I passed her convincingly. As I exited transition two for the 10K run, there she was, shoulder to shoulder with me. We ran together for about half a mile; then she pulled away. About a mile later, I saw her pulled over to the side, noticeably overheated. I silently snuck by in hopes she would not see me. The run course doubled back to the grandstands for the halfway point, and then it was another 5K to the finish back to those same grandstands. Friends and family witnessed Valerie once again shoulder to shoulder with me, and the excitement was huge. Just after leaving the grandstands, I heard Valerie shout out congratulations as she slowed to a walk/jog. I was taking no chances for her to make a comeback and felt super strong for that final leg. My 2:56 finish was supersatisfying and left Valerie serving me beers for the remainder of the day!

Two months later I was in Chicago for yet another Olympic tri. This one was never on my list. However, less than a year earlier after a speaking gig in the Orlando, Florida, area, a guy named Mike had come up afterward and said I had inspired him to take on a triathlon. Often people will approach me after a presentation and tell me they are going to take some type of action. All too often, nothing happens. I had told Mike I would check my calendar and consider joining him. Shortly thereafter, I had seen via social media that he had bought a bike and was regularly training. My calendar was open, and I'd let him know that I was in. Race day arrived, and Mike had signed up for the sprint tri. On race day he must have been at least one hundred pounds lighter than the overweight guy who had come up to me that night in Orlando. Race day was superhot, but we both successfully finished the race. Here, from Mike's story:

> I always get a good laugh when I read or hear Jack tell the story of the day he met Jim Pratt and found his next adventure. The reason this gives me a good laugh is because the real start to my career in sales was the day I shook hands and met Jack Daly at a conference in Orlando, Florida, at the age of twenty-five. I look back on the photo I took that day of Jack and me often to remind myself of just how far I have come mainly because of the systems and processes Jack taught me that day.
>
> The day I met Jack, I weighed in at a staggering 420 pounds, was working well over eighty hours per week, and really did not have any clear direction on where my career was headed. The day I heard Jack speak cleared a fog that was hanging over my career and personal life for far too long. After the conference I had written Jack asking if we could stay in touch, as I was sure I was going to have a lot of questions while I dug through the "Jack in a Box" package of books and training materials I purchased. Thank goodness I did write that note because boy, did I ever have questions, and luckily Jack was there to answer them every step of the way for almost two years.
>
> Two years after I met Jack and wrote that letter, I was watching as my family's company was listed on the Inc. 500 two years in a row, as his teachings gave me the focus I

needed to build and lead a new inside sales team to amazing success. The success in my professional life made me also start to look at my personal life. I was still weighing in at 420 pounds and could feel the burden of all that weight, especially with the stress of our fast-growing business. So I took another page from Jack's book and made a commitment on Facebook that one year from that day, I was going to run and complete the Chicago Triathlon. Mind you, till that point I had never even run a 5K, but I knew that I could do it.

For the next year, I dedicated myself to fixing all the damage I did to my body for twenty-seven years. The next 365 days of my life were some of the most grueling and rewarding days of my life. My public commitment was a constant reminder that I could not give up on this goal, and about four months into it, Jack decided to give me the extra push I needed with a simple note:

"Michael, I am really impressed with your commitment to take back your health and complete your first triathlon. I want you to know I am here rooting for you, and will also be there at the finish line to congratulate you."

That note put my butt in hyperdrive and caused me to take my already ambitious goal to the next level. Remembering Jack's teachings that you need to have clear systems, processes, and accountability, I immediately sought out an endurance-sports training group. The club I found was Chicago Endurance Sports, and after my first meeting with their owner, I knew I had found my solution for all three of Jack's requirements for success. Over the next six months, CES would push me even harder than I was already pushing myself. They also inspired me to compete in multiple 5K runs, a 10K run, and two century (one-hundred-mile) bike rides and be 100 percent ready for my first sprint-distance triathlon that fall.

As fall came around, I was feeling more and more confident about the upcoming triathlon, and knowing Jack was coming, I was determined not to fail at my goal. So I continued to eat right, work out, and control my work schedule through better systems and processes to reduce stress. Then on August 29, 2010, a year after making that life-changing post, I crossed the finish line of a *very* hot Chicago Triathlon at 310 pounds and with a huge smile on my face. If crossing that line was not enough, I also got to share that life victory with Jack, who ran the Olympic-distance triathlon that day, pushing me to look out toward even more ambitious goals ahead.

Today I am proud to say I have completed multiple Olympic-distance triathlons and marathons and, best of all, was able to get my weight down to a manageable 220 pounds. This journey would not have been possible without the inspiration, guidance, and, most importantly, friendship of Jack Daly!

—**Michael C. McMillan**, Chief Revenue Officer, Aceyus Inc.

This is one of my favorite race memories, and Mike McMillan has gone on to Ironman level and is a treasured friend.

Three months later, my family joined me in Cozumel for the week of Thanksgiving and yet another Ironman. This time, sister Valerie decided to step up for her first full Ironman. All the way up until the day before race day, Valerie was expressing real concern over being able to cover the 2.4-mile swim distance. Here I was, giving her swim lessons and tips, the guy who not long ago had been doggy-paddling! Race day arrived, and the excitement was off the charts. We started together, and then I quickly lost her. Since the bike was a two-loop route around the island, I did have the opportunity to see her out there, meaning she had successfully conquered the swim. It was a beautiful layout, and at about the eight-and-a-half-hour mark, I hit the run course, a three-loop out-and-back in the coastal business strip. That was when I saw her again, and she was all smiles. Knowing that running was her strength, I couldn't let up for fear that she would catch and pass me. My 5:15 run brought me close to sub fourteen hours, but I finished a few seconds over. Valerie was all smiles as she crossed the finish line in 15:20, and the family had one of the most celebratory Thanksgivings.

Three months later I headed out for Ironman New Zealand. I'd heard from so many business and triathlon friends how gorgeous Lake Taupo was as a race site. Unfortunately, I couldn't confirm this based on race-day conditions. The torrential rains started the night before and never let up the entire day of the race. Given the conditions I was pretty happy with my 1:23 swim and seven-hour bike leg. The shocker for me was the run—4:51—which was faster than several of my stand-alone marathons. I finished overall at 13:35, and many of my friends wanted to know the secret of that "fast for me" run. The only thing I can surmise is I had enough of the rain and just wanted to get it over with and get under dry cover. Missing out on the beauty of the area compelled me to sign up for next year's race the very next day. Wouldn't you know? A year later the race conditions were even worse, necessitating the race to be delayed a day and converted into a 70.3 distance! So much for the beauty of Lake Taupo!

The year I turned sixty-two saw me finish three full Ironmans, two 70.3 Ironmans, an Olympic tri, and four stand-alone marathons. My final triathlon of the year was a 70.3 Ironman in Myrtle Beach, South Carolina. This race was extra special since the entrepreneur organization I mentioned earlier, Gathering of Titans (GOT), decided to make this a family-participation race weekend. With people racing from the group as well as their friends and family, we had over one hundred people there. Many in the group were inspired by my annual stories of the Ironman racing (we meet as a group once a year), and many were taking the challenge on here. Upon arrival for the race, I discovered that this particular race was an official qualifier for Team USA in the Long Course World Championship. My sister Valerie and I decided we should sign up and see what might happen (nothing ventured, nothing gained). The day before race day, Valerie started bragging to all my buddies at GOT that she was going to "kick my butt." Admittedly, she was well trained, but I was to have none of it. My swim was horrible, and on two occasions, I thought of tossing in the towel but kept pushing nonetheless. I knew she was ahead of me on the bike, but the two-loop track of out-and-back enabled the racers to assess where they stood among all others. I could see her lead was one I could close on and committed to catching her before the run leg. With about ten miles of bike to go, I passed her convincingly, bringing the bike leg in at three hours. On the run the route was such that you could see the others on multiple occasions. Knowing the run was Valerie's strength, I decided to give it all I could early on to rip out her competitive heart. It worked, and I posted my best-ever 70.3 with a time of 6:01. Valerie finished at 6:12, and we both laughed all weekend at the smack talk and the reality. To cap it all off, we both qualified for Team USA, which meant Vitoria, Spain, was a surprise destination in the triathlon journey.

Fast-forward a couple of years, and in April I was at the Augusta Golf Club attending the final day of the Masters. The final six holes with the leaders were in the rain, and the viewing spots were jammed, so I retired to the clubhouse to watch the finish in comfort. While watching Adam Scott do what was necessary for the treasured green jacket, I received an email notice that I had qualified for entry into the Ironman World Championship. Tears of happiness ran down my cheeks as I thought of how special a life I was living and how grateful I was for the many blessings bestowed upon me—witnessing my first Masters and this best Ironman news, pointing to yet another tick on the bucket list!

Six months later, on October 12, approximately two thousand athletes treaded water, awaiting the cannon start at 7:00 a.m. So many of my family and friends were there for the week to share in all the special festivities. As I treaded water, a sense of peace and gratitude swept over me, and I decided that today would be a day of celebration, and to hell with my race times, as long as I met the necessary cutoffs. After all, at sixty-four years old and after learning to swim a short few years before, I was fortunate to be there at all. The cannon blasted, and we were off. The swim in Kona was out and back, and it was purely enjoyable. With about five hundred yards to go to the shoreline, two dolphins showed up and guided me to the swim finish in 1:47. The thought today still produces goose bumps. That 112-mile bike has been long in every Ironman I have raced, and this day was no different. For the first seventy miles, I was tracking to post my best-ever bike performance; then substantial headwinds kicked up, and the final forty-mile stretch was a true slog. When I entered transition two, my bike time came in at 7:12. Not close to my best bike, for sure, but the combo of swim and bike accounted for nine hours, meaning I had a full eight hours to get the run leg complete within the seventeen-hour mark at midnight. I high-fived my friends and family and stopped to let them know that I was going to pretty much walk and occasionally jog the remaining 26.2 and take it all in. After all, this was a day of celebration! My support team was there for me all through the day, and I know what a chore that is. Ironman Hall of Famer and friend John Maclean was out there cheering the athletes on, and we took time for a photo and hug. Sister Valerie got fidgety after the dinner hour and, in the dark of the night, headed out onto the run course to see where I stood. We met up with about eight miles to go. Valerie walked with me for about an hour, then headed back to the finish line to await my arrival. Of special treat was highly accomplished Ironman and friend Mike Wein at the finish line draping my finisher medal over my neck, just after legendary Mike Reilly announced, "Jack Daly, you are an Ironman." All pretty emotional for me.

Several more triathlons would follow that championship race, with a few garnering podium finishes. A couple of years later, the GOT group decided to race the Cedar Point Triathlon in Cleveland, Ohio, in September. Since I had gotten these folks started in the sport, I felt somewhat obligated to register and race. I signed on for the 70.3, and once in the swim, I realized I had slipped in fitness and was really struggling. In fact, within the first one thousand yards, I started to look for a Sea-Doo official to take me in and call it a day. I couldn't find anyone and just turned around and began to swim back to the start and quit. As I swam back, I noticed that the swim in the opposite direction was much easier than the swim out. The swim wasn't going to be as difficult as I had initially imagined, so I once again turned around and headed back to join the others out there. I made the cutoff and proceeded with the fifty-six-mile bike feeling strong and posted a decent bike. The big surprise came when I started the run. A professional speaker friend of mine and GOT group member came out of transition just two ahead of me. David Rendall was my target for the run, and I decided that I would eventually reel him in. It never happened, but the chase resulted in a solid 13.1 at 2:15. I was pooped as I crossed the finish line and headed directly for a chair and a beer with my GOT brotherhood. One of them, Mike Beirne, asked how I did, and I said I had no idea. He pointed to a nearby kiosk that could spit out your results. I told Mike I just wanted to sit and would look it up later. He would have none of that and walked over to claim my results—amazingly I had won my age group! This after nearly quitting seven hours earlier in the swim. This age-group victory qualified me to compete in the US National Olympic Championship to be held in a couple of months. If that weren't enough for the day, at dinner that evening, the GOT members awarded me with a Lifetime Achievement Award, recognizing a number of contributions and accomplishments for the "benefit of the whole."

Two months later I raced my final triathlon (at least for now) at the Olympic Championship in Omaha, Nebraska. I truly lead a "pinch me" life!

TOP 100 GOLF COURSES

In my early fifties, I was gifted the book *Top 100 Golf Courses You Can Play*. The included courses are public courses not requiring a membership and in the United States. Having started enjoying the game of golf when I was caddying at thirteen years old, I dove right into this beautifully packaged book. After just reading thirty-seven pages (the first section was the state of Florida), I added this quest to my bucket list. I figured if I knocked down ten courses a year, the journey would take me ten years to complete. As I write this book twenty years later, ninety-five of the one hundred are complete, and I planned to have already accomplished the final five but was slowed with the challenge of a world confronted with a pandemic. Be assured; those five will eventually get checked off the list!

I shared the book and the idea of knocking these courses down with three close friends, recognizing that we likely wouldn't be able to play all of them together, but we certainly could share several outings. All agreed it was an exciting endeavor. Lifelong best friend Rick Iovine lived on the East Coast, whereas my business partners Gerry Layo and Mark Moses lived on the West Coast, as did I. The year I received the book, I was able to log thirteen on the list, getting off to a robust start. By the end of the next year, I had twenty-four of the one hundred knocked down, and the new listing came out in *GOLF Magazine*. We initially thought that we would work on the original list in the book but quickly learned that every two years, a number of courses get bumped off the list, and other courses are included as new qualifiers. We learned that playing the original list could be near impossible, as some courses flip from public to private status. As well, the new courses added often were more appealing than some on the original list. With these thoughts in mind, we agreed that any courses newly added to the list would be candidates for play and reaching the goal of playing one hundred. As such, "the list" of available courses to choose from grew beyond one hundred, making the quest a bit easier than originally contemplated.

The full list of the ninety-five courses played to date is included in Appendix 7. Twenty-three states were visited, with double-digit courses played in three states (California, fourteen; Arizona, ten; and Hawaii, ten). As for scoring, I've never claimed to be good at the game, just someone who enjoys playing it. Worst score recorded was 102, with a total of five courses in triple digits. Lowest score carded was seventy-nine at Talking Stick (North) in Arizona, the only round in the seventies. Average score was eighty-nine, essentially bogey golf. I'm happy to take that, as most rounds were played on a course for a one-and-only visit.

I was able to combine these golf outings with twenty-one business visits, and in seven states, I also ran a state marathon in the area. Of the ninety-five completed, thirty-four were played on my own, with none of my friends available. Mark joined me on nineteen of the courses, Rick on eighteen, and Gerry on fifteen. Of course, the game of golf is much more fun when shared with friends, but the logistics often necessitated solo play. The good news is that these were Top 100 Courses, so even solo they were typically a great, memorable outing.

While over two hundred readers vote on more than five hundred courses, there were a few courses encountered that left you scratching your head as to how they made the list. Often these courses make the list once, never to appear again. The great news is that most of the tracts are truly world class, and I enthusiastically endorse this journey as a bucket list entry. If you are interested in hearing more, a few of my favorite experiences are detailed in Appendix 7.

PRESIDENTIAL LIBRARIES

As part of my quest to run a marathon in all fifty states, I visited Little Rock, Arkansas. The Little Rock Marathon would be my twenty-first marathon overall and my thirteenth state. The day before the race, I decided to tour the city. The prize was the presidential library of Bill Clinton. It would be my first visit to a presidential library, and I had no idea what to expect. Upon entry there was a welcome video from President Clinton, and it was truly inspiring. Less a library and more of a museum, you could easily spend days reviewing the history of the president from his youth through his presidency. As I made my way through the various exhibits, it felt like a live course on leadership (something on which I have been a lifelong learner). The balance of the day I spent visiting various government buildings and the state capitol. As an added thrill, the next day was race day, and along the route was the governor's mansion, where I felt compelled to have someone take my photo. The race ended at the capitol, where the finishers were presented with "officially" the biggest finisher medal in the sport of marathoning.

Upon leaving the library, I picked up a brochure and learned that there were other similar libraries around the country. Since the visit in Little Rock was so enjoyable, I decided to add the presidential libraries to my bucket list. Completing the official thirteen libraries took me ten years, ending with Herbert Hoover in West Branch, Iowa. With my travels related to my speaking business, combined with the fifty-state marathons and the Top 100 Golf Courses quests, the logistics challenge and opportunity was officially on!

Huge thanks and credit go out to my Business Manager, Jennifer Geiger, who coordinated getting these events to make logistical sense. At times the coordination seemed like a game to us. We would get an opportunity to speak in a certain city, and then Jen would check to see if there was a Top 100 Golf Course, state marathon, or presidential library "in the neighborhood." The definition of *neighborhood* might have been stretched, necessitating a several-hour drive from one event to another (or even a plane ride!). Let's say we were hired to have me speak in a city on a Friday, and we located a presidential library and marathon I needed nearby. I would fly in on a Thursday, speak on Friday, visit the library on Saturday, and finish up with the marathon on Sunday. We would call this the "trifecta of my life," and I'd leave for home filled with gratitude for all I was getting to see and do. Ten of my thirteen library visits were combined with a marathon, a triathlon, or a speaking gig "in the neighborhood."

Presidential libraries give you the chance to experience the events that changed our lives and made us who we are as a nation. The library system began in 1939, when President Franklin Roosevelt donated his personal and presidential papers to the federal government. Each library has its own character, and I found each worthy of my visit. Many are located where the president was raised as a child, and a few even include a tour of the original residence. The learnings I took from my visits included a good grip that many of our country's leaders have come from humble roots, suggesting that anyone can grow up to be president. In some cases, the president and first lady are buried on the grounds, adding to the solemnity.

History truly comes alive at the libraries. Several have exact replicas of the Oval Office, and visitors are encouraged to take a seat at the desk for a classic photo. I was able to walk away with one or more new tidbits of knowledge from every library. FDR is well known for his famous "nothing to fear but fear itself" quote, yet in touring the house where he grew up (and also lived later in life) in Hyde Park, New York, we discovered flame retardants hanging on the walls, as he lived in fear of being trapped in the house should there be a fire. The visit to the Ronald Reagan Library came with the unique surprise of Air Force One in the building, and visitors were encouraged to walk through. Whenever I find myself near a presidential library, I try to squeeze in a visit, as there is so much to see and learn from our nation's leaders.

EIGHT LESSONS FROM VISITING PRESIDENTIAL LIBRARIES

I'm a big believer that success leaves clues, and one efficient route to designing one's own success in life can be through what I call "modeling the masters." Upon reflecting on these presidential library visits, I identified several common threads:

1. Lifelong learning: I was impressed with the love of books that most of these presidents possessed. Beyond being voracious readers, many were writers of books as well. Jimmy Carter, for example, has written thirty-two books and is still stirring up the thinking of nations.

2. Grit: Many of the presidents came from very humble roots; several could be referred to as having started "on the wrong side of the tracks." Family financial hardships were prevalent and led to hard work and effort at an early age. Witness Ronald Reagan, who at age fourteen was a ditch digger, working ten hours a day, six days a week, at thirty-five cents an hour.

3. Commitment: Most came to office with an impressive educational background, doing whatever was necessary to pursue advanced education and leveraging that learning into future successes. Witness Eisenhower, who was desirous of an advanced education, but as the third of seven sons in a financially challenged family, the only route was a military academy route. While the air force was his preference, when he was unsuccessful in getting in, he proceeded to West Point and achieved an illustrious military career.

4. Resiliency: On the way to the position of president of the United States, many of these accomplished leaders suffered multiple defeats in elected office. They bounced back stronger, wiser, and more personally powerful. Examples include Clinton's and Carter's first unsuccessful runs for governor and Nixon losing his run for president by less than 120,000 votes (< 0.2 percent), then losing his run for California governor before victoriously coming back in another presidential contest.

5. Competitiveness: Many of our presidents were active and accomplished sports competitors. I was positively struck by the number of "letter sweaters" on my library tours. While Gerald Ford was routinely the brunt of SNL spoofs for being clumsy (knocking his head on the Air Force One doorway or slicing a golf ball into the gallery), he was a recognized center and linebacker at the University of Michigan, receiving offers from the Packers and the Lions.

6. Process: Having been a Captain in the US Army, I can attest to the foundations of process when it comes to the military. I took note of how many of the presidents had extensive

and highly decorated military backgrounds. Whether it was Carter and his leadership in the nuclear sub program, Bush (41) as a naval pilot, or Eisenhower and his pivotal role in bringing the Allied Forces to victory in World War II (and his burial in military uniform at his request).

7. Decisiveness: Most of these leaders as president were confronted with significant life events, requiring decisions that only they could make. Be it Bush (43) and 9/11, or Kennedy and the Cuban Missile Crisis, or Nixon and Johnson and the seemingly never-ending Vietnam War, or Hoover and the Great Depression, each of our leaders was confronted with big decisions. Imagine Harry Truman and his decision whether to drop the atomic bomb or not (a decision that even today has its detractors and supporters). As Truman said so succinctly by way of the sign on his Oval Office desk, "The Buck Stops Here."

8. Renaissance men: Many of these leaders could lay claim to this designation. Examples of such talent and knowledge are displayed in several disparate fields. Bush (43), upon leaving the office, went on to be a self-taught recognized oil painter. Carter and his woodworking talent manifested in building furniture, and Eisenhower went on to publish a cookbook. Yes, these leaders were open to attempting new things in life, often at a chronological age when many folks choose to think their best days are behind them.

So much to learn from people who have achieved success! If you are a parent, imagine working in concert with your children to sharpen their swords in these eight attributes and begin the process of charting their roads to success (however one chooses to describe *success*).

In addition to the presidential libraries, I was able to add some additional notable visits to foundational places in the history of the United States. Here's a quick look, each checking a bucket list item for me.

1. Mount Vernon, Virginia: While not a presidential library, it was the home of our first president, George Washington, and it has the feel of such a library. Instead of original items, there are replicas, but a visit provides real insight to the challenges and talent of our first president.

2. Johnson Ranch, Texas: I actually learned more about Lyndon Johnson here than I did at his library in Austin. The ranch is a couple of hours' ride outside of San Antonio and well worth the drive. During Johnson's administration, he spent more days conducting the business of the country here than he did at the White House.

3. 9/11 Museum, New York City, New York: A tragic day for the United States and the world. Of all the many sights and things to do in NYC, this is my number one recommendation for those visiting the Big Apple. You could literally spend many days in this place of reverence and respect. I've been back several times, and it is always moving.

4. West Point, New York: As a by-product of my membership in GOT, I met Bernie Banks, one of the senior officers responsible for the education curriculum at West Point. He was gracious to afford me the opportunity of a VIP tour of the school, inclusive of sitting in several classrooms and joining the cadets for lunch in the mess hall. With just a day visit, the quality of the program in producing high-performance officers was abundantly clear.

5. Pentagon, Virginia: One of my clients is led by two long-term and now-retired officers from the army, Paul Trapp and Steve Davis. While we were catching up with one another, I gushed about my visit to West Point, and they asked if I had an interest in touring the Pentagon in a similar VIP fashion. Having lived in the DC area for seven years, I had passed by the building many times. Once inside, I was in awe at the size of the facility, and the tour underscored how big a job it is to maintain our military forces at the performance level they operate in throughout the world.

6. Air Force Academy, Colorado: I combined this visit with my running of the Pikes Peak Marathon and am sure glad I did. The US military academies are open to all US citizens for a visit, as they are "our" academies. Each has its own character, yet all convey a similar message, and that is one of high expectations and professionalism at its very best. We can all learn much from such visits.

7. CIA, Virginia: A truly rare opportunity presented to me from professional speaker Simon Sinek, a close personal friend with ties to the military at the highest levels. You know you are entering a unique venue when you must surrender your mobile phone prior to entry. (My only other occurrence like that was attending the Masters Golf Tournament.) Immediately upon entry you wished that you had it for photos, with that CIA emblem on the lobby floor! My one-on-one VIP tour was beyond fascinating, and touring the private museum was really eye opening. Most surprising was how open my guide was with information and the inner workings of the CIA. If you can ever arrange a visit, this is a not-to-be-missed day.

Many of these opportunities came about by virtue of me being very public with my bucket list and ambitions, coupled with proactive networking. Before this can happen, you first need to wrestle down what's important to you in your life—something I call *life by design*.

PART 2: TIME TO DESIGN *YOUR* LIFE

"But what am I to do?" asked Alice.

"Anything you like," said the footman,
and he began whistling.

—LEWIS CARROLL, *ALICE'S*
ADVENTURES IN WONDERLAND

This is *your* life. You are going to make it what *you* want. First you need to figure out what that looks like and then go after it. With my plan, you will come out ready to live your life by your design.

STEP 1: BIG QUESTIONS

Start the process by asking yourself several provocative questions. This part is called *thinking*. I believe it's the hardest part of the work, and I suspect it's why so few people engage in it. I share with you this note that points to the importance of this in business, but the same importance applies to your knowing where you are going in your own life.

September 2007. YPO Washington, DC, Chapter Retreat.

JD: "Your most important job as CEO is to tell your people where you are going. If I pulled up in front of this resort in a brand-new Ferrari, and you climbed in, what's your first question? Not "Why'd you pick this color?" Not "How fast does this thing go?" No, your first question is, "Where are we going?"

I returned to Washington and wrote a memo to the Walker & Dunlop board telling them I had failed. The memo (which I still have) said I'd been running the company well for three years but that I hadn't set out a bold, clear vision on *where we were going*. I proceeded to lay out the strategy and then developed a five-year growth plan for the company that included growing revenues, net income, and EBITDA 5x in five years. We embarked on that journey not knowing we were just about to enter the Great Financial Crisis. Yet five years later, we had grown revenues ~4.96x, net income ~4.92x, and EBITDA ~5.1x. We truly *got Jack'd*!

Willy Walker
Chairman & CEO
Walker & Dunlop

The questions you consider may vary as you think about your life and desires, but here are some big-picture questions to start you off:

1. What do I want in my life?

2. Why do I want it?

3. When do I want it by?

4. What do I choose to do in order to achieve it?

Wrestling these questions down will take several hours, if not days. The better clarity you get here, the more directly you can make your path to a life by design, the life you dream of! Remember, at thirteen, after I wrestled with these kinds of questions, I came out with this as my guide:

FINANCIAL	PROFESSIONAL
annual income	CEO
net worth	national size
top 25 percent	money business
EDUCATION	**FAMILY**
BS accounting	married
MBA	kids
lifelong learning	

Blank worksheet forms are in the Appendix to be copied and used for these exercises.

At another point in my life, I developed the following "theme" for my year, driven by my big-picture thoughts: Life balance is a priority, continuing to "make a difference" as a professional speaker while enjoying more home life in Southern California. Physical fitness while having fun (bucket list) and world travel is part of such balance.

The better clarity you get here, the more directly you can make your path to a life by design, the life you dream of!

STEP 2: WHERE ARE YOU NOW?

Next up in the process is an honest assessment of where you are currently. Pick the categories that are right for you as you consider your big picture from step 1 and what you want in your life. Here are examples that I have found to be helpful: health/fitness, family, financial, leisure, sport, spiritual, personal growth, business/career, and friends. Choose some, all, or different categories that work for you and your future goals.

Once you have identified the key categories of your life, ask yourself a variety of questions to determine the actions to get where you want to be. This list of questions is not meant to be exhaustive but rather to get you moving in the right direction. Start here, but personalize your questions so that the look inside best reflects *you* and what you need to consider for your goals.

HEALTH/FITNESS:

1. How would I rate my overall health on a scale of 1–10?

2. Am I taking care of myself, generally speaking?

3. How much time am I allotting each week to this area of my life?

4. Am I getting sufficient sleep?

5. Am I following a healthy eating plan?

6. What are some initial ideas to improve in this area?

FAMILY:

1. On a scale of 1–10, how do I rate my relationship with my spouse/significant other?

2. On a scale of 1–10, how do I rate my relationship with my children?

3. On a scale of 1–10, how do I rate my more distant family relationships?

4. What are the strengths in my relationship with my spouse/significant other?

5. What are the areas that can be improved with my spouse/significant other?

6. What are the strengths in my relationship with my children?

7. What are the areas that can be improved with my children?

FINANCIAL:

1. Do I have a financial plan for my family life?

2. Do I operate with a monthly budget?

3. Do I have an age for desired retirement?

4. Have I determined the amount of money needed for retirement?

5. Do I have specific income goals?

6. Do I have debt?

7. If debt, do I have a plan to retire such debt?

8. Am I adequately insured? In what way?

LEISURE:

1. Do I have a desire to read? If so, how often?

2. Do I enjoy movies? If so, how often?

3. What are typical activities spent with the family?

4. What kind of vacations have I been taking?

5. Do I have a plan for vacations?

6. Do I have a bucket list? For myself? For family?

7. What about family meals together—frequency?

8. What are the things I've done with leisure time that provided me the greatest satisfaction?

SPORT:

1. What sports do I enjoy as a spectator?

2. What sports do I enjoy participating in?

3. How often do I participate in desired sports?

4. What sports would I enjoy playing but have yet to carve the time out for?

SPIRITUAL:

1. On a scale of 1–10, how important is this area in my life?

2. On a scale of 1–10, how would I assess my participation here?

3. How would I describe my spiritual life today?

4. What could I improve upon in this area?

GROWTH:

1. On a scale of 1–10, how would I assess myself in this area?

2. What activities have I done in this area?

3. What activities would I like to see more of?

4. What percent of activity is tied to my profession?

5. What percent of activity is tied to my personal life?

BUSINESS/CAREER:

1. How would I categorize the time I have invested in my profession?

2. What businesses/roles have I worked in?

3. On a scale of 1–10, how would I rate my happiness in this area?

4. What would be needed to raise that happiness number?

5. Where is my passion when it comes to career?

6. What stands in the way of improvement here?

FRIENDS:

1. List the names of some old friends.

2. List the names of some new friends.

3. How often do I get together with these friends?

4. Are these get-togethers in person or over the phone?

5. Is this the desired mix of friends and frequency?

6. Do I feel I have too many or too few, or is the mix about right?

7. What could I change to improve this area of my life?

Taking a deep assessment of one's life is not an easy task. The picture we see is often not the one we most desire. The great news is we can change that.

I find it fascinating that people plan their vacations with better care than they do their lives. Perhaps that is because escape is easier than change.

STEP 3: VALUES & TASKS

The following is an exercise I have found helpful in identifying what is most important to me. I've used this tool several times over the past couple of decades. Once again, doing it right requires real "work."

Think about what you value. These values can come from different areas of your life or may be a single set of core values that carry over into the different aspects of your life. Building strong relationships could be a value for you that carries into all aspects of your life. Financial success may be a value that is more focused around your work business even though it has impacts throughout your life. Your values may not include either of these. Consider your own life, what you want it to look like, and what is most valuable to you.

> Consider your own life, what you want it to look like, and what is most valuable to you.

List twelve or more things you value most. Don't worry about the order or priority; at this stage it's about quantity, not quality.

1. _____   11. _____

2. _____   12. _____

3. _____   13. _____

4. _____   14. _____

5. _____   15. _____

6. _____   16. _____

7. _____   17. _____

8. _____   18. _____

9. _____   19. _____

10. _____   20. _____

Now, review the above listing, and circle the top three most important to you.

TASK LISTS

Once you've identified your top three values, create task lists that you would need to complete to successfully integrate these three values into your life.

MOST IMPORTANT VALUE: _____

To-do list:

a) _____

b) _____

c) _____

d) _____

e) _____

f) _____

g) _____

After you have completed the list for your most important value, then move on to the second value, and then complete the third using the same process.

STEP 4: LIFETIME GOALS & TASKS

Next, we move to more of a goal-setting process, listing goals you hope to achieve in your lifetime. Consider what you would like to achieve in your lifetime, and list your lifetime goals. As with your values, it's more about quantity than quality, and the ordering is not important at this stage. There is no right number of goals to include here; you need to determine what feels right for you.

1. _____   11. _____

2. _____   12. _____

3. _____   13. _____

4. _____   14. _____

5. _____   15. _____

6. _____   16. _____

7. _____   17. _____

8. _____   18. _____

9. _____   19. _____

10. _____   20. _____

Now, circle the top three from your list. Following the same process as with the values, create a task list for your top three goals.

MOST IMPORTANT GOAL: _____

To-do list:

a) _____

b) _____

c) _____

d) _____

e) _____

f) _____

g) _____

Complete the process with each of your top three goals.

STEP 5: FIVE-YEAR GOALS & TASKS

Now we want to bring the goals into a near-term focus. Following a now-familiar process, list your near-term goals, those you'd like to achieve in the next five years. Once again, it's more about quantity than quality, and the ordering is not important at this stage, and the number of goals that is right is determined by you.

1. _____   11. _____

2. _____   12. _____

3. _____   13. _____

4. _____   14. _____

5. _____   15. _____

6. _____   16. _____

7. _____   17. _____

8. _____   18. _____

9. _____   19. _____

10. _____   20. _____

Circle the top three from the above listing. As before, run your top three through the task-list process.

MOST IMPORTANT GOAL: _____

To-do list:

a) _____

b) _____

c) _____

d) _____

e) _____

f) _____

g) _____

Complete this for each of your top three five-year goals.

STEP 6: SIX-MONTH GOALS & TASKS

If you had only six months to live, how would you spend them? List your near-term, immediate goals. Again, it's more about quantity than quality, and the ordering is not important at this stage.

1. _____   11. _____

2. _____   12. _____

3. _____   13. _____

4. _____   14. _____

5. _____   15. _____

6. _____   16. _____

7. _____   17. _____

8. _____   18. _____

9. _____   19. _____

10. _____   20. _____

Circle the top three, and run them through the task-list process.

MOST IMPORTANT GOAL: _____

To-do list:

a) _____

b) _____

c) _____

d) _____

e) _____

f) _____

g) _____

One of my treasured lifetime mentors, Jim Pratt, said it so simply and so well: "Focus precedes success." And so I ask you this question: How are you living your life now compared to your answers here?

If you made it this far and put in the work, you have the foundation for tackling your life by design. We will return to this foundation a little later to firm up your route to success.

> It's how you organize your view of the future that determines what the future is.

It's how you organize your view of the future that determines what the future is.

STEP 7: THE BUCKET LIST

Let's take a fun break that will set the table for achieving and experiencing things in life that are unimaginable for most. When I first tackled this, I called it my Life List. When the movie *The Bucket List* was released, I immediately renamed my list accordingly. The concept here, which most are familiar with by now, is making a list of things to do before you "kick the bucket." I've always referred to it as compiling everything I want to do in life before I'm too old to enjoy it. I like the way Harvey Mackay says it: "Don't count the years; make the years count."

> More often, failure in the future is the result of inadequate imagination in the present.

Having a bucket list dramatically improves your life. Clearly from the process we just went through, I'm a big believer in goals. A bucket list helps you keep track of the extraordinary life experiences you seek. All too often people get sucked into getting through their day and their to-do lists, at the expense of injecting the fun into life. People and companies tend to underperform, not meeting their capabilities because they rush to the urgent at the expense of the important.

I regularly pinch myself with the many things I have experienced in my life. Here's just a sampling:

1. Run marathons in all fifty states

2. Run marathons on all seven continents

3. Hike Inca Trail into Machu Picchu

4. Write a best-seller book

5. Fly a jet fighter plane

6. Attend Playboy Mansion party

7. Marathon on the Great Wall of China

8. Golf Pine Valley Golf Club

9. Bungee jump world's largest jump

10. Complete Ironman World Championship

11. Skydive

12. Attend Kentucky Derby

13. Hike Rim2Rim2Rim in Grand Canyon

14. Visit the Great Barrier Reef

15. Visit the presidential libraries

16. Appear on cover of a magazine

17. World travel: Australia, Greece, Russia, China, France, Italy, Spain, Germany, Brazil, Singapore, Peru, Argentina, Dubai, India, Tokyo, London, Ireland, Netherlands, New Zealand, Istanbul, Budapest, Scotland, Africa, Israel, Vietnam, Cuba … and the list goes on.

As you begin thinking about your own goals and what you want your life to look like, do not limit yourself. While there are examples of my bucket lists in the appendices, I think it will be helpful and fun to share some details on several of my favorite bucket list experiences. There are too many favorites to detail here, so if you enjoy these shares, more are included in the appendices. So many of the experiences I have had are genuine *wows*!

1. Marathons in all fifty states: This experience took me thirty-three years to complete if I start counting from my first marathon, or twenty-three years after first putting it on the list. Any way you measure it, the journey took decades. The journey is captured in detail in an earlier chapter, but this one brings great pride in the context of stick-to-ittiveness.

2. Boston Marathon: The idea of running the Boston Marathon was never in my sights, as so many runners attempt to qualify for years with no success. When a client of mine in Boston introduced me to running for charity as a way of experiencing this legendary race, I was in. What a thrill to experience all the celebration in the city for my first Boston Marathon. Yes, *first*, as I went on to run this beauty four times in total. Biggest surprise of all was qualifying in at the age of sixty-two. Getting to share one of those Bostons with my running-crazy sister, Valerie Murphy, was icing on the cake. Special thanks go out to Dan Gould and family for welcoming me into their home in Hopkinton for each of those races, and congrats to Dan (a nonrunner) for joining me in one of the four!

3. Pine Valley Golf Club: Regularly ranked as the number one golf course in the world, it's amazing to me that it's located in south New Jersey, near where I grew up. A client of mine who has grown into being a treasured friend, Tom Londres, made this experience happen for me. (And a bonus was being able to have best friend Rick Iovine out there with me.) I've

now played ninety-five of the Top 100 in the United States and several top courses in the world, and in my opinion, the number one ranking is richly deserved. When I viewed the drone video of the eighteen holes prior to playing, I feared a long, embarrassing day. Happy to report that the day was picture-perfect weather and no embarrassment on the scorecard (yet still triple digits). The pro shop for logo wear was a definite must.

4. Grand Canyon, Rim2Rim2Rim: I've been to the Grand Canyon on several occasions, and each visit is majestic. In fact, my instructions upon my death are to deposit a part of my remains there. When I sit and contemplate the billions of years represented on the wall and realize how small my life is in relation to the universe, it helps me put things in better perspective and realize most of what we get upset over isn't worth the time. Best friend Rick Iovine and I decided to take on the Rim2Rim hike. Starting at the North Rim and hiking down to the base, then traversing the floor over to the south end and scaling the climb up was a dream come true. The day comprised about twenty-five miles in total, about sixty-five thousand steps, and three hundred–plus floors of climbing. All this in heat that reached 115 degrees Fahrenheit. The beer at the end of that evening, after thirteen hours of sunrise-to-sunset hiking, sure was a treat. Five years later, I decided to take the journey on both ways and put the word out to my friend network. Twelve brave souls opted in, and we decided on a September journey. The plus of this month is cooler temps; the drawback is shorter daylight hours. Only four of the group made the return on foot, with the balance of us driving back. My plantar fasciitis acted up

on the first-day south-to-north hike, and since I was running the NYC Marathon in a couple of weeks, I elected to skip the return. The following year I returned with another group of friends and completed the both-ways experience. Everyone agreed that this was truly an epic lifetime event.

5. African safari: To go on a safari once is a true bucket list experience; to go again is pure extravagance. My first was tied in to the Ironman South Africa, and after a week in Port Elizabeth tied to the race, Bonnie and I relocated north by a couple of hours to world-renowned Shamwari. The lodging was truly lifestyles of the rich and famous, and the outings in the wilds were simply jaw dropping. Eight years later, I joined travel queen extraordinaire Marilyn Murphy for a three-lodge Safari excursion in Kenya. The first day alone we experienced more animal sightings than could be expected in the entire trip. However, the best was yet to come. My friend and publisher Adam Witty (traveling with fiancée, Erin) and I went out early one morning, just the two of us and a driver and a tracker. We happened along a leopard's kill of a wildebeest and witnessed the leopard hauling it up into a tree for a big meal. A short while later, a male lion came upon the scene. The lion scared the leopard up the tree, ripped the wildebeest down, and picked up eating where the leopard had been interrupted. With the lion distracted, the leopard was pleased to jump out of the tree and escape with his life. We were no farther than thirty yards from the action, and the tracker said it was the best he had witnessed in ten years as a tracker. Deserved or not, I give credit to Marilyn, as *WOW* experiences seem to be a regular on her trips!

6. Jet fighter plane: One of the beautiful things about a bucket list is the invite to think big and see what happens. To fly a jet fighter sounded like an over-the-top experience, and so I added it to the list. As a professional speaker, I maintain a website at www.jackdalysales.com and regularly post my goals and bucket list on there for the world to see. Less than a year later, I received an unsolicited email from a Wei Chen (whom I didn't know, but he had heard of me as a speaker) asking if this experience was still open. When I replied yes, he sent me a photo of a jet fighter plane he had purchased from the US Air Force. I immediately said yes again, and Wei said we just needed to schedule the when and where. Not long after I met YPO member Wei Chen as he flew into Southern California and picked me up, and off we went into the wild blue yonder. After taking me through some plane acrobatics, he then passed the controls over to me. To this day I'm still amazed at how much life can come toward you if you just put your desires out there. On a sad note, about a year later, Wei had an airplane accident that resulted in his death. Forever grateful to you, Wei.

7. Vietnam/Saigon: I was being groomed to lead troops as an army officer in the Vietnam War. As luck would have it, I was not called upon, but I was always curious as to what Saigon looked like as a city and to experience the infamous tunnels. That opportunity came many years later through my speaking business and an invitation from the international organization Entrepreneurs' Organization (EO). The tunnel experience is burned into my head forever, as I marveled at the ingenuity and intricacies of the tunnel network. I left with a profound sadness in us as humans that we would

resort to such savagery in this war, where so many people lost their lives.

8. Normandy beaches: Bonnie and I were to spend a week in Vitoria, Spain, as a result of me making Team USA for the Long Course Triathlon World Championship. Prior to heading to Spain, we spent a few days in Paris and on a river cruise to the beaches of Normandy and back. With both of our fathers having served in World War II, this visit to Normandy was high on our list. Quite frankly, the sight is visually overwhelming, and the up-close view of where the battles were fought is mind boggling. The quiet respect by all while visiting was appropriate and impactful. Again, sad to see so many fallen soldiers.

9. Taj Mahal: Visiting India for the first time began in New Delhi, again an opportunity presented to me via my speaking business. We allotted sufficient time to visit the world-famous Taj Mahal, and while the several-hour drive was difficult— witnessing so many people living in a stark state of poverty— witnessing the Taj was beyond our expectations. The absolute size was shocking in its enormity, and the grandeur of the property was jaw dropping.

10. Machu Picchu: The queen of exotic travel, Marilyn Murphy, again organized a once-in-a-lifetime tour of Peru for Bonnie and me. While there were many highlights indeed, hiking the Inca Trail and touring the ancient city of Machu Picchu was the ultimate. When I learned that I would be returning to Peru a few years later, I just knew my friend Rick Iovine and I had to share that experience. On my first visit, I was unaware that a special permit was required to climb Mount

Wayna Picchu inside the ancient city. Of just four hundred passes a day, we were blessed to secure two and climbed the mountain the day after taking on the Inca Trail. Not bad for a couple of sixty-eight-year-old guys!

11. Sydney Bridge walk: All of Australia is so special, and if I were to live anywhere other than the United States, Australia would be my choice. I've been fortunate to have seen more of this special country than most Aussies, mostly a result of the many speaking engagements over the past ten years. Among many favorites was the sunset climb of the Sydney Bridge, a safe "daredevil" experience with incredible views.

12. London: My first Ironman was in the United Kingdom, and as a warm-up, Bonnie and I visited London with our great friends Rick and Kathy Iovine for the first time. Since that visit, I've been back many times, often tied to my speaking business. While there is so much history and grandeur throughout the city, my personal favorite is the Churchill War Rooms. Similar to my visits to the presidential libraries, the British efforts in World War II come alive in these underground rooms.

13. Galapagos Islands: This volcanic archipelago in the Pacific Ocean is *the* place for wildlife viewing. Whether on land or underwater, the animals are at total peace with human visitors; it's truly difficult to adequately describe. An incredibly peaceful space on our planet, from which we can learn much.

14. Jerusalem/Israel: Now with Karen in my life (more about this later), I'm provided so many more opportunities to visit new places and experience new things. First on this list was this Middle East city and amazing country. While Karen had previously been here, it was a first for me. Jerusalem is one

of the oldest cities in the world and is considered holy to the three major Abrahamic religions: Judaism, Christianity, and Islam. To visit each section of the Holy City so tightly meshed together and feel the sense of peace and respect was a great takeaway from the visit. To be sure Karen experienced some firsts on this trip as well, my good friend from DC Devin Schain volunteered to join us and engaged a world-class guide. (If you ever visit, the guide is the only way to go!) Among highlights were climbing Masada, a "swim" in the Dead Sea, and, a first for all of us, rappelling. I always work to make a trip or visit a *wow* experience by doing as many new things as possible.

15. Istanbul: Sitting on the Bosporus Strait, this old city of Turkey exhibits the many empires that once ruled there. Visiting the iconic Hagia Sophia with its soaring dome and rare Christian mosaics is truly jaw dropping. Not far from here, the Roman-era Hippodrome is intact with several Egyptian obelisks. The open-air market is a must-see, as long as crowds of people hustling about is not disconcerting for you.

16. Ephesus: Once considered the most important Greek city and trading center in the Mediterranean region, this ancient port city in Turkey is best known for its well-preserved ruins. The condition of the ruins, dating back to the fourth century BC, is simply amazing. Notable names by all visited this great city: Alexander the Great, Mark Anthony and Cleopatra, Julius Caesar, Saint Paul, Saint John, and the Virgin Mary. Favorites for me were the Library of Celsus, the Temple of Artemis, the Coliseum, and the public latrines. Walking the grounds, you can almost see this ancient city as a bustling center of activity.

17. Great Barrier Reef: Most people have heard of the reef, but until you've flown over it, I think its enormity is difficult to comprehend. Covering an area of 133,000 square miles, with 2,900-plus reefs and nine hundred islands, it's one of the seven natural wonders of the world. It is the world's biggest single structure made by living organisms and can actually be seen from outer space. The beauty of the coral and the diversity of fish are without comparison.

18. Pompeii: This ancient city located near Naples, Italy, is one not to be missed. Once buried under thirteen to twenty feet of volcanic ash from the eruption of Mount Vesuvius in AD 79, the city is amazingly intact, and the visitor gets a real feel for life long, long ago. Each visit affords you more learning and appreciation for life.

19. Dead Sea: This salt lake bordered by Jordan to the east and Israel to the west lies fourteen hundred feet below sea level, making it the lowest point on Earth. Surrounded by desert beaches, mineral spas, and oases, the highlight is floating in the sea, as the salinity is so high it's impossible to submerge under the water! Karen Caplan and I have some of the funniest photos from our "plunge" here!

20. Havana, Cuba: My visit was coupled with running the marathon, a unique opportunity to take in 26.2 miles on foot. My friend Howie Kra joined me for this race and city visit, bringing the experience to yet another level. You quickly get the feeling of a city trapped in time. Faded glamour, vintage vehicles, cigar factories—and the old city comes to life with a kind and vibrant people. Special thanks to my friend Susan Leger Ferraro for opening up her residence in

the city and providing us a special driver and guide to give us a real inside look at Havana.

21. *Hyper Sales Growth* book: If you don't stretch, you won't reach. That's a bit how I felt when I put "best-selling book" on my bucket list. Then it became the number one best seller in several categories on Amazon. Special thanks go out to my publisher, and now good friend, Adam Witty, for giving me the push I needed to write this special book.

22. Skydive: In October 2002, my son, Adam, and I jumped out of a perfectly good airplane over the city of Las Vegas. If we weren't nervous before that day, signing all the paperwork and being videoed reading the disclaimers sure would convince the folks on the fence to pass on the experience. We both enjoyed the outing, once we were safely on the ground!

23. Hang glide: I was in Rio de Janeiro as a prelude to racing the Ironman in Florianópolis, Brazil. When I discovered the fantastic hang glide off Pedra Bonita at 510 meters and landing on Pepino Beach, it seemed the ideal location to knock this off the bucket list. These tandem flights include a run off the roof of a building, and for about ten minutes you take in the views of a lifetime!

24. Super Bowl: My first Super Bowl game attendance pitted the Denver Broncos against the Seattle Seahawks, held at the MetLife Stadium in the New York area. The Seahawks defeated the Broncos 43–8, making for a painful fan experience for me, as I was rooting for the Broncos! Best friend Rick Iovine joined me for the week's festivities (as well as buddy Kris Kaplan who jumped in at the last minute), and the entire experience was one for the memory book.

25. Albuquerque Balloon Fiesta: My daughter, Melissa, and her family joined me for this unique experience, long on the list, in 2019. The colorful display of hundreds of balloons taking off to the blue skies together sure had us snapping the photos. What we hadn't anticipated was the early-morning wake-up call to get to the launch site, nor the bone-chilling cold. Nonetheless, it was a real treat to share it with my grandsons Malcolm and Wyatt.

There are so many memorable items I've left out here from the bucket list that have been checked off, even including those detailed in the appendices with my comprehensive bucket list. Hopefully this brief summary will be a catalyst for others to make their lists and begin knocking off some true life experiences. After all, we can design such a life.

Here are a few items on my list yet to be completed:

1. Carry Olympic torch
2. Golf Augusta National Golf Club
3. Hole in one
4. Role in a movie
5. Climb Kilimanjaro
6. Meet a president at the White House
7. Play Top 100 Golf Courses in USA (ninety-five complete)
8. Golf St. Andrews
9. RAAM (Race Across America)
10. Visit Egypt

11. Run with bulls in Pamplona

12. Read fifty-two books in a year

And the list goes on!

One item on my bucket list generates a lot of laughs, then discussion, and that is "live to 125." I put this on the list at twenty-eight years old. At the time, my thinking was that if I lived my life from twenty-eight to seventy-five in a respectful manner when it came to exercise, eating, and living, by the time I arrived at seventy-five, medical science would likely have figured out how to take me to 125. But if I handed the doctors a beat-up old man, they likely would not offer me the necessary tools for the next fifty years. You can imagine the number of people laughing at me over the next forty years, as if this was fantasyland. Yet as we look to the future, a good many people are now expected to cross the one hundred mark! I regularly ask people what age they expect they will live to and then begin to challenge them on a couple of fronts: (1) Why not higher? (2) What stands in the way? and (3) How are they preparing to optimize those years?

On a somewhat sad note, my mother-in-law, Peg Heal, regularly told people that she wanted to live to ninety years of age. When we celebrated her ninetieth birthday in September, little did we know that she would pass away on December 25 of the same year, achieving her self-stated belief she would live only to ninety. So what year will you live to? And what are you planning to do from now until then?

At one point I realized I had completed nearly 90 percent of my list. This is not a list you want to complete! So I typed *bucket list* into my browser and discovered literally hundreds more candidates for inclusion on my list. I picked another fifty to add to my list. Today I average about 75 percent completion of the list—plenty more fun ahead to look forward to!

Now that I have grandchildren, I regularly share my intention to run a marathon with them, hands clasped together as we cross the finish line. This alone compels me to continue to live a healthy and fit life!

For those folks who are married or are in a significant relationship, here is a fun way to take on your bucket list creation. Each person goes into a quiet room for two or three hours, maybe with favorite music tracks playing in the background. During that time, they each write down as many life experiences that seem appealing to them individually. At the end of the session, don't discuss the listing with your mate, thereby building the suspense. The next day, jointly discuss the lists, and negotiate a merged list, working to prioritize the listed items. A further enhancement would be to attach a target date for completion, at least for the top ten or twenty items on the list. For those truly brave folks out there, you could even include the kids in this process and create a family bucket list.

A blank bucket list template is in Appendix 11 for you to get started.

STEP 8: ONE-YEAR PLAN

At this point you have wrestled down what is most important to you and have a clearer view of what you would like your life to be. It is time to take that hard work you did earlier and drill it down with more specificity to create a one-year plan. This plan can take many forms. The key is designing something that will work best for you so you take action. Over the years my one-year plan has evolved into a format I personally find effective for me. It includes a process that increases the probability of my success. I have shared this process with others around the world and have many success stories from those folks. I have shared a few of these throughout the book and am including a few more here:

> Jack, you've had an amazing impact on my life. I'll never forget having you as a guest speaker in our Vistage group, because I'd never met anyone like you. You were the most intense person I'd ever met! At the time we met, I was an entrepreneur and mom of six, with big vision but no tribe and no mentors. My upbringing was fun, but structure and discipline were *not* a part of my family's DNA. You graciously accepted my invitation to meet one on one, as I just wanted another peek into the foreign territory of how thinking bigger and using process, structure, and discipline could help me reach my goals.

The most amazing gift you gave me was access to a whole new world that I never knew existed.... Like your experience as a caddie at thirteen, my eyes were opened to another world that I'd never known existed. Thank you for believing in me, extending your network and support, and being a champion to this Latina mother of six. I will never forget the part you played in helping me to achieve success and find lifelong cherished friendships.

—Theresa Alfaro Daytner

I first met Jack when I was in my late twenties when he gave a presentation about consultative selling to our NY chapter of the Entrepreneurs' Organization. While his presentation about sales and sales management was, by far, the best I had ever heard, at the end of his talk, he mentioned—almost in passing—his process for setting clear, measurable goals and tracking them in minute detail for his personal life to create a life by design.

While I recognized Jack was a truly special person with superhuman willpower I could never match, I was immediately drawn to his clarity of purpose, vision, priorities, goals, and accountability to live his life on his terms and not in reaction to circumstance—a life by design. I approached Jack after his talk and introduced myself to him and asked if he would be willing to share his process with me. He was more than gracious, open, and incredibly generous and excited to "pay it forward." I received a package the following week with photocopies of his entire datebook with his goals and progress tracked in almost maniacal detail. He also included a personal note with some tips and insights about how to live a more intentional life. We had some great conversations, and he provided encouragement and support that aligned with my commitment to myself to live a life with no regrets.

At Jack's suggestion I took time away from my business to work "on" my life rather than just "in" my life and clarified my own purpose, vision, priorities, and goals for the kind of life I wanted to live, which was not nearly the same as Jack's, but I found the process to have universal application. That coaching relationship has turned into a twenty-five-plus-year friendship, and I have been able to live my life with a much greater sense of clarity, purpose, direction, and accomplishment in my life than I had ever thought possible.

Now in my fifties with decades of putting these habits into practice, whenever Jack and I see each other, we always share a knowing look, knowing how fortunate we both are to be "living the dream" every day of our lives. Jack has been one of the most important mentors in my life, and I continue to follow his example by paying it forward and sharing my experience to help others live more proactive and purposeful lives. I developed a forum program and workbook based on Jack's basic principles with my own unique take to help others achieve greater clarity of vision and purpose aligned with goals and scheduling to help others gain the confidence to consciously choose an extraordinary life by living on purpose rather than living by default with regret.

—Damon Gersh, CR
Chairman and CEO
Maxons Restorations Inc.

I met Jack ten years ago while attending his Sales and Management Summit. I benefited from the content and have since woven much of his teachings into the DNA of my firm. Attending his one-day Sales Summit has become mandatory for all new salespeople we hire. He has also worked directly with my leadership team to bring his proven practices deeper into our firm's daily execution. As of late, I hired Jack as a personal coach to help me achieve my top professional and personal goals … On a personal level, Jack has expanded my vision, forced me to ask better questions, challenged things I held too tightly, unlocked areas of fear, ignited untapped strengths, and brought habits of focus, all in a relevant manner with practical application. It would have taken me a lifetime to learn and adopt what Jack imparted to me in a tightly compressed timeframe. Through all of this, I've been given the best gift of all: the gift of his friendship.… For me, Jack has pointed me toward: focus, less and better, grit, endurance, kindness, and "caring about the important." Simply put, Jack has spurred me on to a better me. That's what Jack does. God bless you, Jack Daly. *Go!*

—Tom Londres
Chief Executive Officer, Principal
Metro Commercial

Some of the business-relevant messages have been omitted from these stories to emphasize the focus on using these methods for personal goals and development. There are so many more success stories of people using this process to successfully design their lives.

One of the keys is simplicity. I've included several years of my annual plans in the appendices. Realize I have been using this process over several decades, and as a result, the level of detail I include may be over the top for most people. My suggestion is to keep it simple, and over time you can add more specificity.

I always begin with a theme for the year, reminding myself of the big picture of how I'd like my life to be. The subset categories should support the theme.

Categories important to me include:

1. Family

2. Health

3. Travel

4. Visits with geo-distant daughter's family

5. Golf

6. Bucket list

7. Household

8. Life balance/personal development

As an example, this was my one-year plan when I was sixty-eight.

PERSONAL GOALS—JACK DALY

Theme: Life balance is a priority, continuing to "make a difference" as a professional speaker while enjoying more home life in Southern California. Physical fitness while having fun (bucket list) and world travel is part of such balance.

A. Family

    1. Bonnie

2. Melissa's family

3. Adam

4. Extended family

B. Health

1. Weight (or less) by quarter: 180-177-175-173.

2. No wine unless < 180 lbs (four free days per month). Wine days to be less than workout days.

3. Workouts four to five times per week / 250 a year.

4. Marathons: Forty-nine states completed / eighty-eight total, in quest of fifty states / all continents / one hundred overall. Continents to be completed in May. Fifty states to be completed in October.

   a) Disney Half—January

   b) Surf City—February

   c) DC—March

   d) Great Wall of China—May

   e) Atlantic City—October

5. Triathlons: Asia Ironman will complete all continents, with Malaysia in November.

   a) Oceanside 70.3—April

   b) Maine 70.3—August

   c) Malaysia full—November

6. Swim seventy-two thousand yards / twenty-four hours a year / two hours a month

7. Run seven hundred miles / 132 hours a year / eleven hours a month

8. Bike twenty-five hundred miles / 144 hours a year / twelve hours a month

9. Bike stationary fifteen hundred miles / 108 hours a year / nine hours a month

10. Strength / seventy-two weight workouts a year / six a month

11. Rowing / forty-eight hours a year / four hours a month

12. Blood platelet donations / six a year

13. Doctors: medical—Dec / dentist three times a year / eyes— summer / skin—May

14. Floss daily

15. Water / half gallon daily

16. Sleep / six hours nightly

C. Quality of life / travel / vacations

1. Mexico/Cabo—February

2. Murphy family in California—February

3. Peru/Chile/Machu Picchu—March

4. Family cruise: Caribbean—April

5. Hamilton Island, Australia—April

6. China/Thailand—May

7. Palm Springs—June

8. California beach week—August

9. Iovines in California—August

10. South Carolina golf with Rick—September

11. Nova Scotia—September

D. Visits with the Young family

1. March—DC

2. April—cruise

3. June—Palm Springs

4. July—Charlottesville

5. October—Atlantic City

6. December—Christmas

E. Golf Top 100: Ninety-two total. Goal of four more in 2017.

F. Events

1. Mexico/Cabo

2. Adam's wedding

3. China tours / Great Wall / Thailand

4. Malaysia / Ironman

5. Nova Scotia / golf

6. Ireland / golf

7. Carolina golf / Rick

8. Hollywood sign / June

9. Blimp / June

10. Indoor skydive

11. Segway

12. Bikram hot yoga

13. AcroYoga

14. Publish 2 new books—Shavitz & Bailey

15. Several photo books

G. Household

    1. Sell LaQuinta house

    2. New car—Jack

    3. Investment mgmt. review / twice a year

H. Balance / personal development

    1. Books: thirty per year

    2. Movies: sixty per year

    3. Magazines: twelve monthly

    4. Manage/monitor sleep nights

QTR	1	2	3	4	TOTAL
Business	29	30	27	25	111
Home	47	35	48	43	173
Fun	14	26	17	24	81
Total	**90**	**91**	**92**	**92**	**365**
Meals at home	30	25	36	26	117

135

If you look at my personal goals for any year, it is obvious that health is important to me. Without good health, all other items on my plan are in jeopardy. Notice the degree of specificity. Instead of saying something general like "lose weight," I am specific with a weight target by a specific time period. This then can be measured and gives me a visible target to achieve.

If the annual goal is to run twelve hundred miles, breaking that goal down by mileage per month and hours per month of running sets me up for a short-term target, which will facilitate taking action. Additionally, as I begin to accomplish these shorter-term targets, it provides momentum to continue with the process as well as a spillover of momentum on other goals.

Much of what is in my personal goals for the year is self-explanatory. Let's look at one that begs for more clarity. In the *balance / personal development* section, you can see a *Manage/monitor sleep nights* category. My core business is as a professional speaker, working with audiences all over the world. I enjoy my work immensely and am blessed with demand at such a level that if I let the business dictate what I do, I would be sleeping in hotels for business more than two hundred nights a year, which would not be the life I seek. My home overlooks the ocean in Southern California, and I love the beach. I enjoy world travel and experiencing the world in a fun fashion. In order to strike the desired balance, each year I figure out a maximum number of nights I'm willing to budget for business. I also determine how many nights I want to be traveling for fun and, lastly, how many nights I want to sleep in my own bed.

For many years, the right balance averaged to be about a third each. The last few years, I've desired more home time, coming in near 50 percent and the other two categories at about 25 percent each. Once this is determined, the business nights are budgeted accordingly through the year, and the nights of fun travel are booked and paid for, leaving home for the balance of nights. Over the years these planned nights have turned into actual nights, typically within a 5 percent variance—life by design.

I typically begin the annual planning process in the fourth quarter of each year, with a completion date by mid-December. The final version is usually the result of three or four iterations, with input from my business manager, adult children, and close friends. Once finalized, I forward a copy to five people I call the board of directors of my life. I ask that they each review with me four times each year, comparing actual results to the plan. I'm held accountable to this group a minimum of twenty times throughout the year. A month does not go by where one of them is not ensuring that I'm tracking to the plan. Additionally, I produce a quarterly and annual report to the board comparing actual activities and results to the plan. Examples of several years of these quarterly and annual reports can be found in the appendices.

I recommend everyone select a board to review their progress and hold them accountable. Choose people who care deeply about you personally and will be rigorous in holding you to your plan. This is the definition of accountability—being willing to share your accomplishments (or lack of) can only help you.

Additionally, the process involves tracking and measuring your activity as it relates to the annual plan. I'm fully aware that there are many technological tracking tools, yet I have found a manual tracking process works best for me. There is something about beginning each day recording the actions taken from the previous day that sets a positive tone for the day. This, then, is momentum. The tracking/recording typically takes less than five minutes each day, an hour per month, two hours each quarter, and four hours each year. A small investment of time when compared with the results! A copy of my handwritten tracking process is in the appendices. The tool I use for tracking is an annual planner in the form of a month-at-a-glance calendar. I carry this tracker with me on all my travels and summarize my month, quarter, and year with a simple Word document. The key here is *simple* and *consistent*. I have several friends who were following an automated tracking process and, once they tried the manual method, found it to be significantly more effective. There is research out there that talks about how writing something down creates more retention and better achievement.

My business collaborator Dan Larson summed all this up well:

What have I learned from you?

We all have a choice. What's your vision for the rest of your life?

Decide the game you want to play; set written goals with a clear plan for action and the adventures you want to build into your life at whatever size. Stretch beyond what you think you can, and go for it!

Design balance into your life.

Measure what matters. Accountability is our friend if we are serious about achieving our goals. We all need a coach to hold us accountable to help us get it done.

We can build the life of our dreams when we focus and consistently act with a can-do spirit on the right things that matter most. You've proven it, and live it!

—Dan Larson
CEO, Head Sales Coach
Leverage Sales Coach

For the readers who are business leaders/management, this process should ring familiar. Successful businesses are most often driven by a discipline of tracking, measurement, and accountability. As I've reflected on life, I've often wondered why so many leaders run such successful businesses yet fall considerably short living the personal lives they seek. A few tried-and-true business axioms come readily to mind: (1) things that get measured get done, and (2) inspect what you expect.

> Successful businesses are most often driven by a discipline of tracking, measurement, and accountability.

Once you have built your one-year plan, it's time to stress test the plan before circulating it for comment and input. Some of the self-dialogue could include:

1. What will it take to guarantee I make it happen?

2. What are the possible obstacles?

3. How do I overcome the obstacles?

4. What are the action steps to achieve this goal?

CRYSTAL BALL

A few years ago, I came across a tool that further enhanced my one-year-goal process—the crystal ball exercise. My crystal ball serves as the painted picture of what I want my life to look like that year. Look into a crystal ball, and see your future at the end of next year. Write down what the crystal ball shows you. A great year is ahead!

Step 1: Describe the year ahead based on the crystal ball's prediction. XXXX year has come and gone, and we "rocked" because we achieved the following specific and measurable *outcomes*.

1. _____

2. _____

3. _____

4. _____

5. _____

6. _____

Step 2: What are the top five or six specific and measurable things that made it such a great year? Rank them in order. These are the *activities* that led to the result in step 1.

1. _____

2. _____

3. _____

4. _____

5. _____

6. _____

Refer to Appendix 2 to see a few examples of my previous years' crystal ball results. I've found it helpful to use this tool as a summary of my more detailed one-year plan.

A YEAR IN THE LIFE

One more fun exercise for your consideration is one that I participate in on a five-year basis; for example, I did this the year I turned fifty, then fifty-five, then sixty. The exercise is something I call a *Year in the Life*. During the selected year, I take at least one photo per day. When the year ends, I chronicle my year in a coffee table photo book (thank you, Shutterfly, for making it easy to produce). Since the book will be available for all visitors to my home, I strive to make it a book of *wow*, a book of significance. Since you know in advance when the photo year will be, you can build your personal goals and plans to make the year extra special. I find myself going to bed each night contemplating what my picture will be the next day. Upon waking the next morning, I commit to keeping my eyes open for a photo that might be even better than what I first thought. This entire process has resulted in me "upping my game."

There are some days where the day is such that a single photo is all that is warranted. Then, there are other days that beg for several photos to be taken. When building the book, some pages represent several days, while others warrant several pages for a single day. The photo book is built by month, beginning with a summary of the month, countries and cities visited, epic events attended, and friends and family participants. I frequently hear something like "Gosh, your year represented here is more than most people experience in their entire life!" from people looking through the Year in the Life photo books. Such is a life by design. My most recent book, capturing the year I turned seventy, was filled with so much fun the photo books were produced quarterly. What a life!

These processes have stood the test of time. While I have added various components and details over the years, the basic foundations date back to when I was a teenager. Now, as I look back on a life well lived, I attribute much of my "success" to these processes. I sincerely wish the best in life for you. Time now to take action!

Another reason I take so many pictures and print coffee table books is as I have gotten older, I've noticed that "a picture is worth a thousand words." The photo books help me remember so many experiences I probably would not have remembered.

> One day, an expert in time management was speaking to a group of business students and, to drive home a point, used an illustration those students will never forget. As he stood in front of the group of high-powered overachievers, he said, "Okay, time for a quiz." Then he pulled out a one-gallon, widemouthed mason jar and set it on the table in front of him. Then he produced about a dozen fist-sized rocks and carefully placed them, one at a time, into the jar. When the jar was filled to the top and no more rocks would fit inside, he asked, "Is this jar full?"

> Everyone in the class said, "Yes."

> Then he said, "Really?" He reached under the table and pulled out a bucket of gravel. Then he dumped some gravel in and shook the jar, causing pieces of gravel to work themselves down into the space between the big rocks. Then he asked the group once more, "Is this jar full?"

> By this time the class was on to him. "Probably not," one of them answered.

> "Good!" he replied. He reached under the table and brought out a bucket of sand. He started dumping the sand in the jar, and it went into all the spaces left between the rocks and the gravel. Once more he asked the question, "Is this jar full?"

"No!" the class shouted. Once again he said, "Good." Then he grabbed a pitcher of water and began to pour it in until the jar was filled to the brim. Then he looked at the class and asked, "What is the point of this illustration?"

One eager beaver raised his hand and said, "The point is no matter how full your schedule is, if you really try hard, you can always fit some more things in it!"

"No," the speaker replied, "that's not the point. The truth this illustration teaches us is: if you don't put the big rocks in first, you'll never get them in at all."

What are the "big rocks" in your life?

Your children, your loved ones, your education, your dreams, a worthy cause, teaching or mentoring others, doing things that you love, time for yourself, your health, your significant other.

Remember to put these big rocks in first, or you'll never get them in at all. If you sweat the little stuff, you'll fill your life with little things you worry about that don't really matter, and you'll never have the real quality time you need to spend on the big important stuff. So tonight, or in the morning,

> If you sweat the little stuff, you'll fill your life with little things you worry about that don't really matter.

when you are reflecting on this story, ask yourself this question: What are the "big rocks" in my life? Then put those in your jar first.

PART 3: OBSTACLES & INSPIRATION

The most common characteristic of successful people is that they know where they are going. They are determined to reach their goals and won't let any obstacles discourage them.

OBJECTIONS

As I wrote this book, several folks felt there were some unanswered questions. Having spent decades in the sales arena, I felt these were close to a family we called *objections* in sales. In the interest of getting people to take action and heighten their enjoyment of life, here are some of the more common questions and my responses. I found this to be very fun, and a special thanks goes out to James Ashcroft for nudging me here.

What happens when there is something you are dying to do but life gets in the way (family commitments, work schedules, etc.)?

I don't recall ever having a year where "life" didn't get in the way. As such, the "road to success is always under construction." This could be as simple as planning to finish five marathons in a year and severing my quad tendon in December of the year prior, benching me from marathons until late the following year. I shifted that goal out a year. Or suspending, for the most part, my love of golf for twenty years as I spent more time with my children while they were growing up and living at home. Golf and my quest to race an Ironman were back burnered for those family-formative years. My passion and desires were still alive and kicking; it was just a matter of timing. As such, new items of interest and fun were prioritized.

How do you handle scheduling conflicts? How do you bounce back? Shrug off a bad day? Avoid resentment?

On the big-picture front, I've learned to put things in perspective via an analogy to the Grand Canyon. The Grand Canyon reflects billions of years on its walls, and if I were to live a life of one hundred years of significance, no one could easily find me on the wall. When put in that context, "having a bad year" would be even harder to locate (a bad month, week, day, etc.). This realization really has helped me place life's disappointments in a less frustrating context. Instead of dwelling on the negatives or disappointments, I shift to what I call the *controllables* and make the best of it.

How often do I revisit the bucket list? Any minimum criteria to make the list?

The bucket list is regularly being reviewed and updated. For sure, during the end-of-year process while setting the coming year's goals, the bucket list is reviewed for candidates to schedule for the year ahead. Further, any time I hear of something exciting that's not on the list, out comes the list for another add-on. No minimum criteria, just what I think might be fun to do in life. As mentioned, at one point my list was getting pretty well knocked out, and this was not a list to be "completed." So I searched the web for additional items to add to my list (some as simple as "kiss at the top of a Ferris wheel").

Any advice for those who don't travel for work?

Over the past twenty-five years as a professional speaker, I have certainly been provided with a unique opportunity for world travel. For some, this would be viewed more as a curse than opportunity, and there is no right or wrong here. Since travel has always been on my list, it made eminent sense for me to enter the professional-speaker profession. That said, if travel opportunities are less prevalent in one's life, then their bucket list would reflect this. If travel is desired, the choices of where and when will require more thought and planning. Beyond travel, there are plenty of exciting things to do in life. With all my international travel, one of my favorite two weeks of travel was 100 percent by car, visiting a variety of places throughout California with good friends.

What have all your travels and experiences taught you that you can pass along?

Our planet is a big place with so many unique and exciting sights to see. While there are many cultural differences as you weave your way through countries, the thing that pops out even more is the many things we have in common with each other. Kindness is found everywhere. With each trip I've made, I've always returned home with an added sense of gratitude for all I have and am blessed with. The absolute breadth and depth of poverty is striking, yet the people who are not as blessed as I am exude an incredible amount of warmth and kindness to their fellow person. Despite the many world challenges, the world is a kind and good place.

How did you deal with low-motivation periods in your life?

I hope my answer is not viewed as Pollyanna, but I don't recall ever having a low level of motivation. I primarily attribute this life advantage to the *Life by Design* process. The focus goes straight to the yearly plan, capturing the controllables for action and moving forward with progress. The process provides plenty of motivation and enthusiasm.

How did you bounce back after some of your early disappointing results?

As with the previous answer, it's all about recommitting to a fresh list of actions. It's about "moving forward." One example is a whole year that certainly handed me more than my share of disappointments: severed quad tendon resulting in no running for nearly six months; malignant melanoma cancer requiring significant head surgery; COVID-19 pandemic, wiping out a significant income stream and all travel. As the year progressed, it was about rebooking events when the calendar facilitated and pivoting the business accordingly. Writing this book was a result of that year and my recommitment process when hit with the obstacles. I had planned to write this book but not yet budgeted the time.

How do you maintain focus on your goals? Do you look at a list daily?

Having followed my *Life by Design* process for more than fifty years, it's now like breathing to me. More like a good habit. I carry my goals with me everywhere and look at them every day, sometimes more than once a day. Additionally, I have my accountability team, my board of directors of my life, each running through the list with me at least four times per year. I also report to myself and the board in a written summary quarterly. Lastly, I record daily all activities related to the goals.

Any advice you can provide to people who aren't wired like you to still access these processes?

I certainly realize that people are different, yet I believe these processes can work for all, at some level. There is no right or wrong here. Many people don't have the appetite to take on as ambitious a list as I have, and I get that! My late wife, Bonnie, was one of those individuals. Early in our relationship, I attempted to "win her over" to my way of goal pursuit. Her personal style shied away from written commitments and outside accountability. Her joys in life were more often tied to her children and me and where we wanted to go in life. However, when she determined a goal of importance to her, she shared it with me and asked that I support her in her effort. Otherwise, she deferred to my goals. The processes work, regardless of the depth and breadth of an individual's goals.

How important do you believe an emotional commitment is when it comes to goal accomplishment?

I've spent my professional life in the sales arena. One of the constants to success is a sales professional's belief in the product/service represented. If you don't believe in it, you won't be successful at selling it. I feel this is true with the goal process as well. Additionally, accomplishments don't come easily. They require a commitment to work. In a word, I call it *grit*. Grit and belief are emotional components and are integral to success in the pursuit of the life we design.

THEN, LIFE HAPPENS

So let's get real. While I stand steadfast in my belief that one can truly design their life, it doesn't always roll out according to the design. I've encountered many bumps in the road on my life journey. We may not be able to avoid the bumps, but we can steer our course in response to them.

Early in pursuit of my professional goals, I worked for the same company for ten years, gradually working to achieve my goal to be president of a national financial services company. Nine years in, when I was thirty-four years old and only two steps removed from the CEO position, in a surprise heard round the business world, well-known corporate raider Victor Posner swooped down and seized the Fortune 200 company where I worked in an unfriendly takeover. I felt as if my designed life was irreparably ruined. I was ordered to meet directly with Victor within the first couple of months, at his corporate location in Miami Beach, Florida. After a tense six-hour meeting, he declared that he "liked me a lot," and he wanted me to become a part of his inner circle of business leaders in what he called the "Victor Posner Empire." On one hand, this seemed like a dream come true, as I would be responsible for running several national businesses of his two–hundred–plus portfolio. Financially, my life would be "set."

However, in quick order I discovered this dream was actually a nightmare. I discovered that my values were in clear conflict with those of Victor Posner's. While so much of my life was driven by business successes and financial accomplishments, I learned that values trumped money and position. I declined his "attractive" offer and found myself without a company and paycheck. I was a husband and dad with attendant responsibilities, and the stress was considerable. This ushered in my adult years of entrepreneurialism, and I have been forever grateful for this unplanned entry of freedom, fun, and impact. While I subscribe to living a life of intention and goals, I've also discovered that life has a way of throwing curveballs, and one's drive requires resiliency and navigation. From there I would go on to build several more successful businesses, pen a few best-selling books, and impact many people in a positive fashion along the way.

Another bump in my professional road came later in life. Imagine winning Entrepreneur of the Year honors and ranking on the Inc. 500 list as the tenth-fastest-growing company in the United States yet having to downsize the company from 275 people to thirty-five in a single day later that same period due to swiftly changing market conditions. Today, that company has resurrected itself and is bigger than ever.

In my pursuit of Ironman race goals, I had a freak bike fall while training, resulting in a broken elbow. My "designed" race had to be missed, but I snuck in a replacement race once recovered. A year later, yet another bike accident, this time resulting in a broken collarbone, seventeen stitches in my head, and a concussion. Once again, the "designed" Ironman race had to be canceled and replaced with a later race.

Family "designs" were not always smooth either. In his twenties, my only son, Adam, had become addicted to meth. I'm happy to report that after several difficult years battling the addiction, Adam is healthy, drug-free for seventeen years and counting, and a terrific contributor to society. Goals and plans were "redesigned." My only daughter, Melissa, was diagnosed with cancer at forty-one years old and, during a lengthy hospital stay, had to battle deadly sepsis. Certainly not envisioned in my life by design, and today we celebrate her life resurgence as a cancer survivor. My wife of forty-seven years, Bonnie, was diagnosed with stage 4 pancreatic cancer at sixty-six years old. After a valiant fight with the killer disease, she passed away later that same year. Once again, not configured in my life by design.

After completing my ninety-fifth marathon in Havana, Cuba, in November, I had a freak one-step fall on a step, resulting in a severed quad tendon in December. My life by design called for five marathons that year, with number one hundred in Athens, Greece. The injury scrapped my entire race schedule for the year.

At seventy years old, I was diagnosed with stage 3 malignant melanoma on my head, operated on that month, and am now happy to report cancer-free. Certainly not contemplated in my life by design.

The world was confronted with the coronavirus, and COVID-19 has impacted us all in a full-force pandemic. Travel shut down, group gatherings for business or races all paused. Again, damaging to my contemplated life by design.

These bumps in the road are just a sampling of what I call *shit happens*. The key is to confront the challenges and redirect your energy to the controllables in your life. When constructing your life by design, recognize that there will be unexpected challenges. The key is to bounce back and redesign accordingly.

I can't change the direction of the wind, but I can adjust the sails to always reach my destination.

—Jimmy Dean

It's less important how many times you may get knocked down in life; the key is to get back up quickly and move forward. That is a real-life version of life by design!

MY SEVEN IRONMAN
LESSONS LEARNED

Several years ago, I wrote the Amazon number one best seller *Hyper Sales Growth*. In the conclusion, I shared life lessons that I captured on my journey completing an Ironman triathlon. I thought summarizing those here would bring a good finish to launching you on to your life by design.

I find a lot of the same themes in both the Ironman sport and the sport of sales and sales management. Growing oneself and growing one's business have much in common, as I have learned in my journey. These same lessons apply to designing your life.

Attitude is central to success. Fifty percent or more of success in life is a head case. It has to do with getting up in the morning and saying, "Give it everything that you've got." If you bring that to your life, you have the differentiated advantage.

LESSON ONE:

Vision. You can't get there unless you know what "there" is. Craft your life as you would like it to be, a life that excites you.

LESSON TWO:

Goals/playbook. Commit to your goals by putting them in writing. Add specificity in terms of timelines and tasks required.

LESSON THREE:

Practice. Often to get to our desired end zone, some practice is needed. Do it.

LESSON FOUR:

System of measurement. Things that get measured get done.

LESSON FIVE:

Bring on a coach/mentor. Here we are looking for someone to hold you accountable as well as someone who can be helpful in assisting you on your journey.

LESSON SIX:

Health/wellness. Our behavior has a significant impact on our health. A healthier "you" will have that much more to enjoy in life.

LESSON SEVEN:

Attitude. We get to choose, positive or negative. I've never understood those who choose to be negative.

So what is *success*?

One summer I was fortunate to play several rounds of golf at Pebble Beach and struck a bond with my caddie. We both shared time in the military, and I suspect that facilitated a regular and easy conversation each time on the course. One day he recounted a story to me that has stayed with me ever since. My caddie spent twenty years in the military and then retired on a military pension. He was an avid golfer (index range from −1 to +1) and a member of the military Bayonet Club, a terrific course not far from Pebble Beach. Two to three times each week, he would caddie at Pebble to pick up a few bucks and meet interesting people while walking the inspiring links. This pretty much summed up his life.

Once each year Pebble Beach would host a high-profile golf tournament sponsored by a Fortune 500 company, and my caddie was on the bag of that company's CEO. As they walked the beautiful course in splendid weather, the CEO mentioned that this was his favorite week of the year, the week he would get to spend at Pebble Beach. For the most part, the balance of his year was spent with the responsibilities and stresses that come with such a position. As my caddie was recounting this story, we were walking along the fourteenth fairway, a challenging par-five dogleg to the right, graced with magnificent estate properties. My caddie then pointed to one of those houses and noted that it was owned by a widow from Houston. She spent the majority of her time at her home in Houston and visited the Pebble Beach house for just a few weeks a year. During the times of her absences, she hired my caddie to house-sit the property, so he got paid to live in a mansion on the Pebble Beach course.

With that, he turned and grinned at me, asking me who I thought was "more successful." With that, we smiled at one another and walked to the next shot.

Here's to you and your journey. A journey I call *Jack Daly's Life by Design*.

WHAT'S NEXT?

Remember the question: Are your best days behind you, or are they ahead of you? Well, for me that's easy, as my best days are ahead.

I'm often asked by family, friends, and people I run into by way of my speaking business, "When are you going to retire?" To me it's a funny question. I'm seventy-two years old and love what I do professionally—making a positive impact on businesses and people's personal lives. Most of this work is from the stage at conferences. As long as the people in the seats perceive me as "relevant" and worth listening to, and as long as I enjoy the travel and stage experience, why would I consider stopping? In many ways I pinch myself over getting paid to do what I love so much. At the same time, I am a realist. Do I see myself doing this at one hundred years old? Likely not. How about at ninety? Again, likely not. When I ask, "How about at eighty?" Well, that is getting too close to me today, and I'd like to believe I can go to at least eighty! Heck, Warren Buffett is ninety, and Richard Branson is seventy-one, both doing much better than I am financially, and they are still at it. Why not me?

When I lost Bonnie to cancer, I was sixty-eight years old. I'd never been on my own, as I went from living at home with my parents until the day of marriage to sharing life with Bonnie. While my life was well lived, I was at a true loss as to what life would be like going forward. Oh, sure, I had my goals, my bucket list, and a thriving speaking career. I had plenty to keep me busy, and busy I like! I was positioned to continue to make a positive difference in people's lives.

I enjoyed married life; I enjoyed sharing life with another. It took me more than a year of drifting to finally resolve that my life was full. The likelihood of finding someone my age who would embrace such a life (well-traveled, fully engaged in business, intensely physically active, a packed bucket list) as well as my shortage of competencies on the home front (and well-honed personal peculiarities) was likely slim to none. Yet if someone showed up in my life who could embrace or tolerate such a companion, I'd be energized to welcome such a person into my life.

Then, in my early seventies (nearly two years after Bonnie had passed), at dinner in a restaurant with a twenty-plus-year CEO client, as we got up from the table, we kissed. Where that came from will always be a life mystery. Karen and I had shared many a dinner together over the years, often me with Bonnie and Karen with her husband, but nothing ever in the realm of a kiss! Within weeks we agreed that with each other being single, we should pursue the concept of life together. Yes, we did go through that age-old process of terms of engagement. Yes, we covered the potential hurdles in such a relation-ship. And we went straightaway to work on merging our bucket lists and goals. Karen said it better than I ever could, so: "Bonnie and I grew up together; Karen and I will now grow old together."

With Karen now in my life, we are operating as a powerful team to suck the marrow out of life together. We experienced a magical trip to Israel, which provided an exciting preview of life ahead together, and we are now busy planning to take down our merged bucket list.

Just a quick glance of my yet-to-be-completed bucket list portends much in the way of excitement. Carrying the Olympic torch and meeting a president of the United States in the White House are just two that will get anyone's heart rate off and running!

It's just about *design* and *execution*.

A PERSONAL NOTE FROM KAREN CAPLAN

I met Jack when he spoke to my CEO group in 1997. His talk on sales was so motivating that I chased after him as he was leaving and asked him for his business card. I told him I wanted to have him come speak to my sales team at my company.

I first invited Jack to talk to my team of more than twenty about sales and customer service. He was so energizing that I invited him back three or four more times over the next twenty years. Over the years, he and his wife, Bonnie, and I shared a few dinners, and I always felt lucky to be invited to their annual holiday party at their home, as I got to mingle with their many friends and successful business colleagues.

After Bonnie passed away, we continued our annual dinner together, catching up on our lives and travels. I remember thinking, "Gosh, I wish I could meet someone like Jack." And later I found out, he was saying the same thing to himself: "I wish I could meet someone like Karen." You see, we were truly just friends and business associates. Over the years, during his speaking gigs at my company, he had called me out for not pushing hard enough to achieve our goals and, in fact, said my company goals were too low. I appreciated his "kick in the ass" approach, even though my employees who witnessed our banter were horrified.

And then, at a dinner together on August 18, 2019, after a bit of wine, we got up to leave, and we have no idea what happened. But there we were, face to face. And we kissed.

And, as they say, the rest is history. After our business-only relationship for twenty years, we realized we had so much in common. A zest for life, a drive to succeed, and a love of travel and entertaining. In less than six months, we decided to start living together.

So imagine my life now: I live with one of the top speakers in the world on sales, sales management, and CEO coaching. As we recap our day each evening, I witness firsthand how passionate he is about making a difference in people's lives. For the dozen or so clients he has at any one time, he treats their businesses as if they were his own. When he is prepping for a live or virtual gig, it's the same. He is all in. A day does not go by without him sharing a Facebook post, an email, or a text message from a client who has been positively impacted by Jack's energy, advice, and passion.

If you are reading this, you have just finished this book. Just know that everything Jack recommends is real, it works, and anything is possible if you have a desire, set a goal, create a plan, and follow it.

I've been Jack'd!

XOXO
Karen

Karen B. Caplan
President and CEO
Frieda's Specialty Produce

BOOKS BY JACK DALY

Hyper Sales Growth

The Sales Playbook for Hyper Sales Growth

Paper Napkin Wisdom

Coaching Companies to Greater Sales & Profits

Daily Sales Motivators

Marketing Magic

Real World Sales Strategies That Work

Real World Management Strategies That Work

Mastering the Art of Success

TO CONTACT JACK DALY

Jack regularly delivers keynotes, workshops, and training in the areas of Life by Design, Sales, and Sales Management. Additionally, he coaches CEOs around the world and facilitates the Sales Manager Forum.

More information and tools can be found on the web at **www.jackdalysales.com** and **www.jackdalyslifebydesign.com**

Or, contact us at **888-298-6868**, as well as email at **jack@jackdalysales.com** or **jennifer@jackdalysales.com**.

PERSONAL GOALS 2017—JACK DALY

Theme: Life balance is a priority, continuing to "make a difference" as a professional speaker while enjoying more home life in Southern California. Physical fitness while having fun (bucket list) and world travel is part of such balance.

A. Family

    1. Bonnie

    2. Melissa's family

    3. Adam

    4. Extended family

B. Health

    1. Weight (or less) by quarter: 180-177-175-173.

    2. No wine unless < 180 lbs (four free days per month). Wine days to be less than workout days.

    3. Workouts four to five times per week / 250 a year.

    4. Marathons: Forty-nine states completed / eighty-eight total, in quest of fifty states / all continents / one hundred overall. Continents to be completed in May. Fifty states to

be completed in October.

   a) Disney Half—January

   b) Surf City—February

   c) DC—March

   d) Great Wall of China—May

   e) Atlantic City—October

5. Triathlons: Asia Ironman will complete all continents, with Malaysia in November.

   a) Oceanside 70.3—April

   b) Maine 70.3—August

   c) Malaysia full—November

6. Swim seventy-two thousand yards / twenty-four hours a year / two hours a month

7. Run seven hundred miles / 132 hours a year / eleven hours a month

8. Bike twenty-five hundred miles / 144 hours a year / twelve hours a month

9. Bike stationary fifteen hundred miles / 108 hours a year / nine hours a month

10. Strength / seventy-two weight workouts a year / six a month

11. Rowing forty-eight hours / four hours a month

12. Blood platelet donations / six a year

13. Doctors: medical—Dec; dentist—three times a year; eyes—summer; skin—May

14. Floss daily

15. Water / half gallon daily

16. Sleep / six hours nightly

C. Quality of life / travel / vacations

   1. Mexico/Cabo—February

   2. Murphy family in California—February

   3. Peru/Chile/Machu Picchu—March

   4. Family cruise: Caribbean—April

   5. Hamilton Island, Australia—April

   6. China/Thailand—May

   7. Palm Springs—June

   8. California beach week—August

   9. Iovines in California—August

  10. South Carolina golf with Rick—September

  11. Nova Scotia—September

D. Visits with the Young family

   1. March—DC

   2. April—cruise

   3. June—Palm Springs

   4. July—Charlottesville

   5. October—Atlantic City

   6. December—Christmas

E. Golf Top 100: ninety-two total. Goal of four more in 2017.

F. Events

   1. Mexico/Cabo

   2. Adam's wedding

   3. China tours / Great Wall / Thailand

   4. Malaysia/Ironman

   5. Nova Scotia/golf

   6. Ireland/golf

   7. Carolina golf/Rick

   8. Hollywood sign—June

   9. Blimp—June

  10. Indoor skydive

  11. Segway

  12. Bikram hot yoga

  13. AcroYoga

  14. Publish two new books—Shavitz & Bailey

  15. Several photo books

G. Household

   1. Sell LaQuinta house

   2. New car—Jack

   3. Investment mgmt. review / two times a year

H. Balance / personal development

   1.   Books: thirty per year

   2.   Movies: sixty per year

   3.   Magazines: twelve monthly

   4.   Manage/monitor sleep nights

QTR	1	2	3	4	TOTAL
Business	29	30	27	25	111
Home	47	35	48	43	173
Fun	14	26	17	24	81
Total	**90**	**91**	**92**	**92**	**365**
Meals at home	30	25	36	26	117

PERSONAL GOALS 2018—JACK DALY

Theme: Life balance is a priority, continuing to "make a difference" as a professional speaker and CEO coach while enjoying more home life in Southern California. Physical fitness while having fun (bucket list) and world travel is part of such balance.

A. Family

   1.   Melissa's family

   2.   Adam's family

   3.   Extended family

B. Health

1. Weight (or less) by quarter: 180-177-175-175.

2. No wine unless < 182 lbs (four free days per month). Wine days to be less than workout days annually.

3. Workouts four to five times per week / 250 a year.

4. Marathons: Fifty states completed / ninety-six total; marathon all continents; one hundred overall total goal. Continents to be completed in May; fifty states to be completed in April.

   a) DC—March

   b) Charlottesville—April

   c) Cape May, NJ—April (That's fifty states!!)

   d) Great Wall of China—May (That's all continents!!)

   e) Berlin, Germany—September (will be four of the world's Big Six)

   f) Catalina Island ECO Marathon—November

   g) Others as present selves on calendar

5. Triathlons: Not of emphasis this year. As calendar presents opportunity.

6. Swim seventy-two thousand yards / twenty-four hours a year / two hours a month

7. Run seven hundred miles / 132 hours a year / eleven hours a month

8. Bike two thousand miles / 120 hours a year / ten hours a month

9. Bike stationary five hundred miles / thirty-six hours a year / three hours a month

10. Strength / ninety-six weight workouts a year / eight a month

11. Rowing / forty-eight hours a year / four hours a month

12. Blood platelet donations / five a year

13. Doctors: medical—January and July; dentist—three times a year; eyes—summer; skin—May

14. Floss daily

15. Water / half gallon daily

16. Sleep six hours nightly

C. Quality of life / travel / vacations

1. Ireland—January

2. Maui—February

3. China—May

4. Cape May family reunion—May

5. Australia—July

6. Asia—August

7. Grand Canyon—September

D. Visits with the Young family

1. March—DC

2. April—Charlottesville

3. May—Cape May

4. Various—open opportunities

5. December—Charlottesville

6. Open—Long weekend with the grandsons

E. Golf Top 100: ninety-three to date / target goal of ninety-seven

F. Rejoin golf club; play fifty rounds

G. Events / bucket list

    1. Ireland

    2. Maui

    3. Super Bowl if Eagles in

    4. China tours / Great Wall

    5. Climb to Big Buddha—Hong Kong

    6. Fiftieth state marathon

    7. All-continents marathons

    8. Pine Valley Golf

    9. Rim2Rim2Rim

    10. Indoor skydive

    11. Attend boxing match

    12. Bikram hot yoga

    13. AcroYoga

    14. Shear a sheep

    15. Visit Hoover Dam

    16. Several photo books

H. Household

    1. House improvements / enhancements

    2. Investment management review / twice a year

I. Balance / personal development

    1. Books: thirty per year

    2. Movies: sixty per year

    3. Magazines: twelve monthly

    4. Manage / monitor sleep nights

QTR	1	2	3	4	total	%
Business	26	21	18	14	79	22%
Home	50	40	59	63	212	58%
Fun	14	30	15	15	74	20%
Total	**90**	**91**	**92**	**92**	**365**	

PERSONAL GOALS 2019–JACK DALY

Theme: Life balance is the goal, marrying my quest to "make a difference" as a professional speaker and CEO coach while enjoying a mix of more time at home, exercise as a staple to include added emphasis on golf, world travel, and continuing pursuit of the bucket list.

A. Family

    1. Relationship with Leslie

    2. Melissa's family

    3. Adam's family

    4. Extended family

B. Health

1. Weight (or less) by quarter: 185-183-180-180.

2. No wine unless less than 185 lbs (four free days per month). Wine days to be less than workout days annually.

3. Workouts four to five times per week / 250 a year

4. Marathons: Currently at ninety-three, goal of one hundred total, a few in 2019

   a) Surf City: Feb 3—94

   b) London: Apr 6—95

   c) Berlin: Sep—96

   d) Others as opportunity presents

5. Triathlons—not of emphasis in 2019

6. Swim seventy-two thousand yards / twenty-four hours a year / two hours a month

7. Run twelve hundred miles / 240 hours a year / twenty hours a month

8. Bike one thousand miles / sixty hours a year / five hours a month

9. Strength / ninety-six weight workouts a year / eight a month

10. Rowing / thirty-six hours a year / three hours a month

11. 3.6 million steps / three hundred thousand monthly / ten thousand daily

12. Sit-ups / fifty daily / fifteen hundred monthly / eighteen thousand annually

13. Yoga / one day a month

14. Blood platelet donations / five per year

15. Doctors: medical—Jan and July; dentist—three times a year; eyes—summer; skin—May

16. Floss daily

17. Water / half gallon daily

18. Sleep / seven hours nightly

C. Quality of life / travel / vacations

   1. Cruise: Bahamas and San Juan Puerto Rico—Jan

   2. India—Mar

   3. Sri Lanka—Mar

   4. Dubai—Mar

   5. Copenhagen—Mar

   6. Vegas—April

   7. London—April

   8. Asia—May

   9. Hawaii—Jun

   10. Calgary—Jul

   11. Australia—Jul

   12. Prague/Paris—Aug

   13. Cruise?—Aug

   14. Kenya—Sep

   15. Berlin—Sep

16. New Mexico—Oct

17. Napa Valley—Oct

18. Cabo—Nov or Dec

D. Visits with the Young family

1. April—Charlottesville

2. June—California

3. Oct—New Mexico

4. Dec—Charlottesville

5. Various as windows of opportunities present

6. BHAG—long weekend with grandsons

E. Golf

1. Top 100—has ninety-five complete; more in 2019 as presented

2. Play forty rounds

3. New clubs

4. Lessons

5. Index to twenty

F. Bucket list / events

1. Cruise Puerto Rico/Bahamas

2. India

3. Copenhagen/Denmark

4. London

5. Golf St. Andrews

6. Masters attend

7. Super Bowl if Eagles in

8. PGA Bethpage

9. Oahu, Hawaii

10. Vegas/James Taylor

11. Asia

12. Calgary Stampede

13. Brother Joe and Sandy visit for a week to CA

14. Australia

15. Prague/Paris

16. Kenya/Safari

17. New Mexico Balloon Festival

18. Napa Valley wine tasting

19. Jerusalem

20. Attend boxing match

21. Bikram hot yoga

22. AcroYoga

23. Shear a sheep

24. Hoover Dam visit

25. Several photo books: photo a day plus others as present

G. Household

    1. Backyard enhancement

    2. Investment management review twice a year

H. Balance / personal development

    1. Books: thirty a year

    2. Movies: seventy a year

    3. Magazines: twelve monthly

    4. Sleep nights/balance

QTR	1	2	3	4	Total	%
Business	44	28	16	15	103	28%
Home	31	41	42	66	180	50%
Fun	15	22	34	11	82	22%
Total	**90**	**91**	**92**	**92**	**365**	

    5. Handwritten note of one or more per day

PERSONAL GOALS 2020—JACK DALY

Theme: Life balance is the goal, combining my commitment to "making a difference" as a professional speaker and CEO coach while enjoying a mix of more time at home nurturing a new relationship in my personal life. World travel will continue to be a priority, while pursuit of my bucket list and exercise as a life staple are key components in providing balance to my professional pursuits.

APPENDIX 1: PERSONAL GOALS SAMPLES

A. Family

   1. Relationship with Karen

      a) Monthly dinner with family/friends

      b) Monthly "dress up" dinner

      c) Outside runs together

      d) Shared gym time

      e) Movies together (6)

      f) Reagan/Nixon libraries

   2. Melissa's family

   3. Young family

   4. Extended family

B. Health

   1. Weight (or less) by quarter: 180-178-178-175.

   2. No wine unless less than 182 lbs (four free days per month). Wine days to be less than workout days annually.

   3. Workout four to five times per week / 250 a year

   4. Marathons: Due to broken leg on December 5, my five scheduled marathons will shift to 2021. Goal is one (unspecified) in 2020, pending doctor's green light.

   5. Run three hundred miles / sixty hours

   6. Bike one thousand miles / sixty hours

   7. Strength / ninety-six weight workouts a year / eight a month

   8. Rowing / twenty-four hours a year / two hours a month

9. Two million steps / 167,000 a month / 5,500 a day

10. Distance on foot / one thousand miles a year / eighty-three a month

11. Sit-ups / fifty daily / fifteen hundred monthly / eighteen thousand a year

12. Yoga / one session monthly

13. Restart blood platelet donations / two for year

14. Doctors: medical—Jan and July; dentist—three times year; eyes—summer; skin—twice a year

15. Sleep / seven hours nightly

16. Floss daily

17. Water / half gallon daily

C. Quality of life / travel / vacations

1. Cabo 2/15–20

2. Grand Canyon 2/21–23

3. NYC 3/19–23

4. Prague/Paris/London 4/30–5/15

5. Toronto 5/27–28

6. Long Beach Island 5/28–6/6

7. Australia/NZ 7/17–8/2

8. London/Dublin 10/12–18

D. Visits with the Young family

   1. June—Long Beach Island

   2. Open—Southern California

   3. Sept—DC

   4. Dec—Charlottesville

   5. BHAG—long weekend with grandsons

E. Golf—complete Top 100 (at ninety-five now) by August 2020

F. Bucket list / events

   1. Write / publish "life" book

   2. Napa wine country 7/10–13

   3. *Hamilton*—NYC—March

   4. PGA Tourney—SF 5/15–18

   5. Long Beach Island 5/28–6/6

   6. Top 100 golf (5)—August

   7. Ryder Cup—Wisconsin 9/25–27

   8. Iovines outing—open timing/event

   9. Marlin fishing—Cabo—Feb

  10. Catalina Island

  11. Wrap a snake around neck

  12. Kiss on top of Ferris wheel

  13. Have palm read

  14. Super Bowl if Eagles in—Feb

15. Hot-air balloon

16. Attend boxing match

17. Bikram hot yoga

18. Reagan/Nixon libraries

19. Hoover Dam visit—Feb

20. Several photo books

G. Household

  1. Sell house

  2. Buy house

  3. Move

  4. Investment mgmt. review—twice per year

H. Balance / personal development

  1. Books: thirty a year

  2. Movies: eighty a year

  3. Magazines: twelve monthly

  4. Handwritten note of one or more every other day / 180 total for year

  5. Sleep nights / balance

    a) Business 100 27%

    b) Home 170 47%

    c) Fun 95 26%

    d) Total 365 100%

Note: Due to my broken leg in December 2019, many of my health/fitness goals have been materially reduced from prior years, as physical therapy will be the first half of year priority. By second half of 2020, goal is to be at prior-year run rates. Bring on the decade!

APPENDIX 2:
CRYSTAL BALL EXAMPLES

DATED AND WRITTEN DECEMBER 2017:

JACK ROCKED IN 2018:

1. Physical fitness: If we aren't healthy, nothing else matters.

2. Family time: Fun times with those closest to you.

3. New business endeavors: CEO Coaching & Sales Manager Forum.

4. World travels: Combo business and personal, along with bucket list.

5. Return to golf interests: Top 100 and local club.

6. Bucket list pursuits: Add to list and knock off current list.

INDICATORS:

1. Weight 175–180; races as detailed in one-year goals; exercise levels totaling at least five hundred hours; Cape May Marathon—fifty-state celebration; Great Wall Marathon—all-continents celebration; Berlin Marathon for number four of Big Six.

2. Family reunion at Cape May; Rim2Rim2Rim; Maui; grandkids long weekend; Melissa and Adam family events.

3. Expand CEO coach to fifteen clients; expand sales manager forums to at least two groups, ideally four groups; leverage strategic alliances; *JD Magazine*.

4. Ireland; Maui; Great Wall/China; Australia; Asia; Grand Canyon; Germany.

5. Rejoin golf club; play at least fifty rounds; Top 100 from ninety-three to ninety-seven.

6. Bucket list including marathons in all fifty states; marathons in all continents; Great Wall of China; skydive indoors; shear sheep; boxing match; Big Buddha; Rim2Rim2Rim; Hoover Dam; Bikram yoga; AcroYoga. Others as they present themselves.

DATED AND WRITTEN DECEMBER 2016:

DALYS ROCKED IN 2017:

1. Physical fitness: If we aren't healthy, nothing else matters.

2. Family time: Fun times with those closest to you.

3. New business endeavors: Establish and reinforce passive revenue streams and brand.

4. World travels: Combo business and personal, along with bucket list.

5. Return to golf interests.

6. Bucket list pursuits.

INDICATORS:

1. Weight 173–180; races as detailed in one-year goals; exercise levels totaling five hundred hours; Atlantic City Marathon—fifty-state celebration; Great Wall Marathon—all-continents celebration; Malaysia full Ironman—all-continents completion.

2. Valerie Murphy family visit week; Iovines CA visit weeks; Adam wedding week; cruise with kids/grandkids; home nights = 170.

3. Launch Sales Manager Forums; leverage strategic alliances; enhance online initiatives; optimize Forbes Partnership; launch *JD Magazine*; two coauthor book launches.

4. Mexico adventure; cruise Caribbean; China/Great Wall/Thailand; Australia twice; Malaysia beyond Ironman; Machu Picchu/Chile.

5. Top 100—another five to ninety-seven; Hamilton Island, Australia; South Carolina trip with Rick; Ireland; Nova Scotia; some local Southern California.

6. Bucket list, including marathons in all states; marathons in all continents; Ironman in all continents; Great Wall of China; blimp ride; Hollywood sign; skydive indoors; Segway; Bikram yoga; AcroYoga.

APPENDIX 3: YEAR-IN-REVIEW SAMPLES

REVIEW OF 2018 PERSONAL GOALS

STATS:

	2018	2017
Exercise days	246	242
Wine days	237	208
Exercise hours	396	390
Run miles	1,055	722
Marathons	3	2
Strength hours	105	106
Bike miles	63	1,216
Rowing hours	44	59
Blood platelets	8	8
Golf rounds	15	7
Top 100 Golf	2	1
Air miles	150,420	120,954
Number of flights	104	108
Speak gigs	64	84

	2018	2017
Books	26	29
Movies	112	64
Nights home	198	245
Nights for business	76	79
Nights for fun	91	41

HIGHLIGHTS:

1. Memorial for Bonnie in Cape May, along with weeklong family reunion

2. Leslie surprisingly arrived in my life in June

3. World travel—Ireland twice, Beijing, Australia, London, Berlin

4. Two cruises in Caribbean

5. Rim2Rim2Rim in Grand Canyon

6. Maui week, lots of activities

7. Great Wall of China Marathon for seventh continent

8. Fiftieth state marathon in New Jersey

9. Number one Pine Valley golf course

10. Potato Chip Rock twice

11. Rejoin golf club Marbella

12. Rod Stewart concert

13. Patron at the Masters

14. Hot-air balloon in Australia

15. Kayak Vancouver

16. Hike mountain in Vancouver

17. Copter through Chicago tour

18. *Love* (Cirque du Soleil) in Vegas

19. *Absinthe* twice in Vegas

20. *Wicked* in San Diego

21. Temecula wine country

22. Christmas celebrations on both coasts

COMMENTARY:

Instead of losing ten pounds to 175, ended year at 186. Workouts on plan. Big accomplishments with fiftieth state marathon and Great Wall of China Marathon for seventh continent. Significant shortfall on both swim and bike goals, as triathlons were zero point of focus. Strength and rowing goals on plan. Blood platelets over plan, making a difference. All doctor visits, floss/water, and sleep goals met. World travel as planned. Visits with the Young family on plan. Getting close on Top 100 Golf Course goal; nailing Pine Valley was a biggie. Rejoined golf club (Marbella) and took four golf lessons. However, goal of fifty rounds underachieved by a lot with fifteen rounds. More emphasis in 2019. Several bucket list items knocked off the list, and those do not carry over to 2019. Several house improvements completed. Books close to plan, and movies more than double plan. Nights for business were on plan, and actually shifted some home nights to fun nights when Leslie arrived in my life (June).

Overall, a successful year and look forward to 2019. A full life, a blessed life, a life by design.

YEAR IN REVIEW 2016—JACK DALY

DEC 31, 2016

For those readers new to this annual write-up, this is my summation and reflections on the personal side of my life, similar to a board of directors report in the business world. As noted in last year's report, Bonnie declared I was overextending myself, and as I reflected on the year, I agreed to scale it back a bit. At the same time, I noted that the year would be jammed with more than most would be willing to venture out on. Both were accomplished.

Before reviewing my personal happenings, a quick recap of the family. Sadly, over the Christmas holidays, Bonnie's mom, Peg, passed away. She lived ninety healthy years, of which I knew her for more than fifty, and we were fortunate to have her close by in California for the last few years. Grateful for the years we had. Looking ahead, we are focused on June 2017, as son, Adam, became engaged to "his" Melissa, and the wedding is in June. Our grandsons Malcolm (8) and Wyatt (4) continue to grow in so many ways and will be joined by Jake with the big wedding. Daughter Melissa's health all points to a positive direction, and Bonnie and I celebrated our forty-seventh wedding anniversary. Time flies!

So I call it *life by design*, and I've been practicing it for decades. I hope readers of this report are personally encouraged to "step up their game" and reach for their dreams. They are truly in reach.

HIGHLIGHTS:

Tough to pick an opener, but moving to our new home that we had been eyeing for a decade sure has to rank up there. Took the opportunity with the move to build a custom wine cellar, which is fully stocked with one thousand bottles, so come by and visit. Of course there were plenty of marathons, which will be noted later, but traveling to Greenland with Mark Moses and running the Polar Circle Marathon certainly makes the highlight reel! Published my third book in three years (titled *The Sales Playbook*) with Dan Larson and now can lay claim to *number one Amazon best seller* three years running. Pursuit of my bucket list recorded so many "ticks of the boxes": Phoenix Open with stadium seating on hole sixteen with Rick Iovine; Kentucky Derby with Adam Witty and my Business Manager, Jennifer, and her husband, John; Ryder Cup with host Lane Gold; Mount Rushmore; Dubrovnik visit; gondola ride in Venice; dogsledding in the Arctic; Barossa wine retreat; stadium roof walk in Adelaide with Jim Moularadellis; glacier and icebergs in Greenland; golf on some of world's finest in Tasmania, Australia, Ireland, and the United States; Pompeii ruins; and completion of my tour of the presidential libraries. Grateful to have my supportive wife, Bonnie, with me on so many of these adventures.

BALANCE:

Thirty-plus years ago, we moved to weather-friendly Southern California, which we enjoy immensely. Yet I'm here less than half the time, as I jet around the world with my speaking profession and personal pursuit of my bucket list. Left unchecked, I could find myself "hotel caged." Years ago, Bonnie and I agreed to decide in advance the number of nights away from home as a max, and my Business Manager, Jennifer, does a great job orchestrating the calendar accordingly. We decided to increase the number of nights home in 2016, and the good news is 168 in 2017 (and the plan was 157) versus prior year actual of 121. Here's a historical look at how it works.

YEAR	2017	2016	2016	2015	2015	2014
	Plan	Actual	Plan	Actual	Plan	Actual
Business	111	107	111	131	125	146
Home	173	168	157	121	131	138
Fun	81	91	98	113	109	81

The plan of optimizing a combo of business and personal travel was the key to execution here. As can be seen of a review of the above stats, for the most part, things that get measured get done. The highlight was not just more days at home than planned, but year-over-year comparison was a net gain at home of forty-seven days—or 39 percent improvement in that desired metric. Goal in 2017 is a similar performance, with several at-home vacations planned with friends/family.

Health/fitness: Fitness results in 2016 were a mixed bag—some highs, some lows, and an overall improvement from 2015 yet shy of prior years when I had Ironmans on my calendar. I've targeted one full Ironman and two 70.3 Ironmans in 2017, so overall exercise levels should go up. Overall exercise hours were nearly one hour per day with a total of 356 hours compared with last year's 283.

On the racing front, it was nine overall marathons, bringing lifetime tally to eighty-eight in my quest for one hundred. Of those nine, six were new states, bringing state total to forty-nine (New Jersey is the missing state, which will happen in October). Surf City Marathon was the first of the year, which made for a full weekend for Rick and me, as we spectated at the Phoenix Open the day before. The following weekend I raced Mississippi Marathon, a point-to-point raced in 26.2 miles of headwinds. Mike Wein and Susan Haag were

YEAR	2013	2012	2011	2010	2009	2008
	Actual	Actual	Actual	Actual	Actual	Actual
Business	138	109	117	119	101	132
Home	142	179	151	188	175	141
Fun	81	81	98	68	78	83

out there running Atlanta Marathon for my state number forty-six. (Mike is a world-recognized age-group performer in the Ironman sport, and Susan logged her one hundredth Ironman in 2016.) In May I squeezed in local OC Marathon and a new state—Fargo, North Dakota—where I was joined by Andy Heck (always great to have company!). My favorite 70.3 Ironman in Honu was raced, albeit where I pretty much walked the run, as I was truly fatigued. Scenic Montana Marathon was next, followed three weeks later in Omaha, where I qualified and competed in the USA National Olympic Triathlon Championship. (I was way back in the pack, whereas speedster Mike Wein was near the front!) Three weeks later I found myself in a Roswell, New Mexico, marathon, which was really lonely with fewer than fifty marathoners in total on an out-and-back route. Bonnie rooted me on in South Dakota for state number forty-nine in early October, just as that part of the country was closing down for the cold winter weather. Fun visit to Mount Rushmore and Crazy Horse Memorial was the bonus here. Two weeks later, it was Mark Moses and I knocking out the Polar Circle Marathon. With the first 10K on an ice cap base and knee-high snow, coupled with an all-day race of minus twenty degrees and twenty-eight-miles-per-hour winds, it is now my number one favorite marathon of the eighty-eight lifetime. No intention to ever race it again, but one hell of an accomplishment and lifetime memories! Special note was the goal of running one thousand miles in the year, which was accomplished Christmas Eve with my grandsons at the finish. 2017 plan is to wrap up all fifty-states marathons, all-continents marathons with the Great Wall of China in May, and an Ironman on all continents in November in Malaysia. Big stuff there! Summary of key stats follows:

YEAR	2017	2016	2016	2015	2015	2014
	Plan	Actual	Plan	Actual	Plan	Actual
Exercise days	250	222	225	184	225	242
Run hours	132	200	160	170	160	152
Run miles	700	1,000	1,000	893	1,000	974
Bike hours	252	79	130	61	180	154
Bike miles	4K	1,129	2K	954	2K	2,464
Swim hours	24	3	36	8	36	32
Swim yards (km)	72	6	100	21	100	87
Strength	72	74	60	35	60	69
Rowing (hours)	48	–	–	–	–	–
Total hours	528	356	386	273	436	407
Wine days	200	250	175	206	175	181

YEAR	2013	2012	2011	2010	2009
	Actual	Actual	Actual	Actual	Actual
Exercise days	228	240	245	268	254
Run hours	142	133	170	171	102
Run miles	728	785	1,056	930	585
Bike hours	183	251	178	220	222
Bike miles	2,858	3,992	2,855	3,463	3,903
Swim hours	35	43	51	87	76
Swim yards (km)	100	125	157	260	218
Strength	65	66	81	99	93
Rowing (hours)	–	–	–	–	–
Total hours	427	498	480	577	493
Wine days	169	173	156	143	178

Weight maintained acceptable delta to 180 year round. Big step up in hours and exercise overall planned for 2017, reflection of tracking bike on both outside and stationary, goal of rowing added, and commitment to racing another full Ironman. Five hundred twenty-eight hours is a step up over the past couple of years but consistent with prior Ironman years. It's all about commitment. This step up should result in desired weight loss of around ten pounds. Increased planned wine days is more planned time at home combined with new wine cellar. Cheers and balance!

Doctor visits were all completed according to goal, each with positive reports. Blood platelet donations were eight, compared to goal of five. This is significant for me, as each visit positively impacts on average three people's lives. Lifetime donation count now over two hundred. Water intake and flossing on plan, and backed off the "shakes," as no material improvements seen last year as a result. Overall sleep hours per night have improved to an average of six per night, although big variances with travel schedule. Note as well, too many sick days during the year, as well as periods of exhaustion, so need to stay alert about overextending myself.

Family / grandparenting from afar: Kids living on both coasts, with their own adult agendas; grandkids with their school and activity schedules and living on opposite coast; and a world-traveling schedule sure provides its challenges to family time. We celebrated Christmas twice, a week apart on each coast, thereby getting to see all. The Youngs visited us for a week on the California beaches, which was terrific but too short. As well, we linked up as the calendar and travel provided. This will continue to be an ongoing challenge, requiring work and coordination by all in the family. The upcoming wedding and a family cruise, as well as year-end holidays, will all enhance 2017 in this regard.

Travel: As is customary, the actuals pretty much fall in line with plan, as most is booked a year or more in advance. One hundred sixty-eight air flights were logged in 2016, compared with 170 in 2015. That represented 219,991 miles, compared with 216,157 miles in 2015. Fun fact is always my personal car mileage—4,126 miles this year compared to 2,420 miles. (As Bonnie reminds me, you can't log many when you aren't home!) World travels were show-stopping: Amsterdam magical; Dublin, Ireland, pure fun; two visits to Australia, one with Bonnie, where we were hosted by our good friends the Moularadellis and ventured to our favorite Barossa wine country; my first visit to Tasmania, and it surely won't be my last; returned for second visits back-to-back years to Kuala Lumpur and Singapore, and I can never get enough of those (special note that I took on the stinky fruit—Durian—hosted by George Gan); tremendous hospitality shown to me by EO in both Panama (where we private-flight toured over the canal) and Nova Scotia; bike toured Copenhagen on way to Greenland; a relaxing week on the Big Island of Hawaii, built around Ironman 70.3; plenty of stops throughout North America; the lifetime memories of Greenland, with dogsledding, ice fjords, etc.; and sharing a truly special trip with Bonnie to Venice, Rome, and a cruise along the Croatian coast (including so many great stops such as the Pompeii ruins and Dubrovnik, to name a few).

And to think that 2017 schedule has more bucket list visits in store!

Catchall: I played double-digit (eleven) rounds of golf for the first time in years, whereas I used to play triple-digit numbers of rounds. This was enough to get the golf bugbite, so I now plan to up the rounds in 2017. Of the eleven rounds played, three were on the Top 100 in the United States, bringing me to ninety-two on the list of one hundred. As well, several more of the rounds were on the Top 100 of the World list. The Phoenix Open with the infamous sixteenth hole was a total hoot. More like a four-day Woodstock concert experience, where I'm convinced many never saw a single golf swing! The Kentucky Derby was a longtime bucket list that got checked off, and it's always fun to hold the winning ticket ("costumes" were all you've ever thought of, and then some). Visiting the presidential libraries has turned out to be one of the more fun excursions I've taken on (each with its uniqueness and oddities). The Ryder Cup was so much fun that I believe I will be a regular when it's in the United States and possibly when in Europe as well. (Note, golf like you've never experienced, particularly on the fans' side of the ropes.) Touring Venice, Italy, is a lifetime highlight, and Bonnie did it right with reservations at the Hotel Gritti. Murano glass visit and purchase, gondola ride, and historic visits were a few notables. Windstar Cruises are always living a life of the rich and famous (at least for a week!). A weather challenge on the route provided us a bonus stop in Pompeii ruins, which was mind boggling. Every port was a wow! Rome is Rome (can never get enough!). Back in the States, we really marveled at Mount Rushmore. I'd love to tell you about my private tour of the CIA headquarters (thanks to my good friend Simon Sinek), but if I shared, I'd have to eliminate you. Suffice to say, it was special. And then there was Greenland and that North Pole Marathon. (Stop by our house and see the customized photo book; a picture is worth a thousand words.)

I read thirty-eight books, compared with goal of twenty-four, and watched eighty-seven movies, compared with a plan of sixty. (Remember—lots of air flights.) The plan was to have 104 home-cooked meals, and Bonnie outdid herself cooking up 112, another contributor to my few pounds of weight gain. Plan for 2017 has been upped to 117. (Hey, more nights at home, seems only fair.)

My personal goals for 2017 are posted in a separate document; suffice to say, they are equally ambitious. (Life is to be lived!) Additionally, my business plan and highlights are covered separately, and there are quite a few exciting new endeavors scheduled there as well. My speaking gig count was managed to ninety-one for 2016, managed down from the 113 of 2015. For 2017, the plan count is one hundred.

Summary: I'm grateful for the life I have and the people I count as friends. I'm privileged to be able to share my experiences with others so they might elevate their lives and businesses. I'm blessed with good health and a robust business. Excitedly looking forward to 2017, and hope to see many in my travels.

THIRD QUARTER 2014 REVIEW

HIGHLIGHTS:

What a life! And where do I start? Family reunion of a week at Long Beach Island, two Top 100 Golf Courses, three triathlons, two wine-country visits, James Taylor concert, 9/11 Memorial visit, and the list goes on! Perfect weather for our return to Long Beach Island after thirty years away, hosting family aging from two to sixty-five. Week included a marriage proposal, the Cast House lodging with ten bedrooms, and so much family fun and bonding. Top 100 Golf Courses—now played at eighty-four, picking up Atlantic City Country Club, where terms *birdie* and *eagle* were started, and also the legendary Bethpage Black in New York, which was every bit as challenging as noted for. The NYC Triathlon was superfun, with a Hudson River current assist, posting a sixteen-minute swim, and an all-around great race—I will be back for this again. Following month was Santa Barbara Triathlon, one of the world's oldest, nearing a Half Ironman distance. Major bike crash with two miles to go (no broken bones, just broken bike) yet posted the fastest run in age group, just missing the platform finish. (It was also the annual GOT race, making it even more special.) Next month, it was Olympic-distance tri in San Diego, placing first in age group (too funny, only in age group and oldest competitor in the race!). Temecula and Santa Ynez wine-country visits were both fun and unique. Day before the Long Beach Island reunion, several of us took in my favorite James Taylor concert, always a highlight and fun to share with several friends/family. The 9/11 Memorial visit was surely touching and moving and should be on everyone's to-do list, so tastefully done. Baseball-park visits continued, with great seats at Wrigley Field for one hundredth anniversary and final home game for the Padres. Great progress made on next book with my partner Gov, *Paper Napkin Wisdom*, hoping for a publication near year end. All this while suffering from more days sick in a quarter than I can ever recall!

Weight unchanged at 180. Hit the wine hard this quarter with wine country and increased time at home. Throughout nine months, 132 days vs. 120 same time last year. Workout days close to same, 186 vs. 194 year prior, ahead of plan of 168. Exercise hours at 311 vs. 341 a year ago, reflecting my being sick of late, near plan to date. Run miles/hours were 766/115 vs. 592/117 last year and plan of 750/120. Bike was 1,932/122 vs. 2,265/145 last year and plan of 2,475/165. Swim was 65K/23 vs. last year's 73K/26 and plan of 90K/36. Strength at fifty-one, same as prior year vs. plan of forty-five. Clearly, enthusiasm has waned for the triathlons, and racing looking to be curtailed in 2015, with more emphasis placed on marathons.

Books read at fifteen vs. plan of eighteen, as emphasis placed on writing *Hyper Sales Growth* and *Paper Napkin Wisdom*. Movies at fifty-seven vs. plan for forty-five, reflecting plane movies. Have gotten more into my golf, now at ten rounds, with several world-renowned tracks. Blood platelets donation at three, shooting for four by year end. Air mileage was 133,695/119 flights vs. 145,075/128 flights last year. Car mileage near nonexistent at 1,896 year to date, less than the 2,326 last year! My bike mileage alone is now ahead of it!!

Business nights away at 107 vs. 110 last year and plan of ninety-eight. Home nights at 102 vs. ninety-eight last year and plan of 102.

Fun nights away at sixty-four vs. sixty-one last year and plan of seventy-three. All within an acceptable range.

I'm thankful for the life I get to live and the generally speaking great health I enjoy.

APPENDIX 4:
JACK DALY'S BUCKET LIST

*Completed items are starred.

1. Ironman*

2. Ironman—all continents*

3. Marathon—all continents*

4. Marathon—all fifty states*

5. Boston Marathon*

6. Run marathon < four hours*

7. Ironman < fourteen hours*

8. Antarctica Marathon*

9. Ironman World Championship Hawaii*

10. Ironman 70.3 World Championship Clearwater*

11. Race car on track*

12. Hang glide*

13. Skydive*

14. Bungee jump—first and largest*

15. Golf Augusta

16. Golf Cypress

17. Golf Pine Valley*

18. Golf Pebble Beach*

19. Attend Ryder Cup*

20. Hole in one

21. Golf with high-profile pro golfer

22. Attend the Masters*

23. Golf St. Andrews

24. Play in a Pro-Am Golf Tourney

25. Play Top 100 Golf Courses in United States

26. Attend US Open Golf Tourney*

27. Run Great Wall Marathon*

28. Alcatraz Triathlon

29. Catch marlin deep-sea fishing*

30. White-water raft in Idaho*

31. Attend NCAA basketball finals*

32. Climb a mountain of note*

33. Attend Kentucky Derby*

34. Attend Olympic event

35. Bike ride across United States

36. Eco-Challenge

37. Hang glide / parasail*

38. Cruise Mediterranean*

39. All Hawaiian Islands*

40. Grand Canyon*

41. Vegas, baby*

42. Fall season in New England*

43. California wine country*

44. Explore Australia*

45. Greek islands*

46. Athens, Greece / Acropolis*

47. Alaska cruise and midnight marathon*

48. Russia: Moscow / St. Petersburg*

49. China*

50. France: Paris / Eiffel Tower*

51. Explore Brazil*

52. Wine country, Italy

53. Wine country, France

54. Madrid, Spain / Portugal

55. Singapore*

56. Peru / Galapagos Islands*

57. Argentina*

58. Dubai*

59. Mardi Gras*

60. Taj Mahal (India)*

61. Munich, Germany*

62. Tokyo*

63. Windsor Castle*

64. London exploration*

65. Rome exploration*

66. Cancun*

67. Bermuda*

68. Caribbean cruise*

69. Barcelona*

70. Florence, Italy*

71. Cruise Danube*

72. Venice*

73. Netherlands*

74. Egypt/pyramids

75. Milford Sound / New Zealand*

76. Yosemite*

77. Niagara Falls*

78. Ayers Rock / Outback Australia*

79. India*

80. World Trade Towers, NYC*

81. Vatican / St. Peter's*

82. Vienna, Austria*

83. Stratford-upon-Avon*

84. Colonial Williamsburg, Virginia*

85. Great Barrier Reef*

86. Barossa wine country, Australia*

87. Daintree Rainforest*

88. Istanbul*

89. Ephesus, Turkey*

90. Budapest*

91. Dublin, Ireland*

92. Edinburgh, Scotland*

93. Empire State Building, NYC*

94. Officer in military*

95. BS and MBA degrees*

96. Become an A-list speaker*

97. Set up Adam in business*

98. Write business book*

99. Write book on my life journey

100. Celebrate fiftieth wedding anniversary (forty-seven and Bonnie passed)*

101. African safari*

102. Ride in a jet fighter plane*

103. Rock & Roll Hall of Fame*

104. Regular platelets donor > one hundred times*

105. Sydney Bridge walk*

106. Hot-air balloon ride*

107. Have a role in a movie

108. Playboy Mansion visit*

109. Visit NY and Chi-X trading floor*

110. DC: Smithsonian and Capitol*

111. Visit presidential libraries*

112. Play blackjack at Monte Carlo Casino*

113. Meet a president at White House

114. Sleep in a castle*

115. Kiss the Blarney Stone*

116. Own a second home*

117. Meet David Copperfield with Adam*

118. Be active grandparent*

119. Leave 15 percent estate to charity

120. Live to 125!

121. Stand under the Hollywood sign*

122. New Year's Eve in Vegas*

123. Grand Ole Opry / Nashville *

124. Zion National Park*

125. Pike Market—Seattle*

126. Original Starbucks*

127. Visit White House*

128. Changing of the Guard at Buckingham Palace*

129. Sunset in Santorini*

130. Tour a windmill—Holland

131. Climb to Big Buddha—Hong Kong

132. Soak in Blue Lagoon—Iceland

133. Hear pope speak at Vatican

134. Make a wish at Trevi Fountain—Italy*

135. Leaning Tower of Pisa*

136. Ride a Vespa in foreign country*

137. Explore Van Gogh Museum—Netherlands*

138. See Gaudi's La Sagrada Familia—Spain*

139. Hear the call to prayer at Blue Mosque—Turkey*

140. Albuquerque Balloon Festival*

141. National Cherry Blossom Festival—DC*

142. Walk on a black-sand beach*

143. Meet a world leader*

144. Attend a boxing match

145. Attend a film premiere*

146. Attend a murder-mystery dinner*

147. Eat in a blindfolded dinner gala*

148. Be a game show contestant

149. Be on the cover of a magazine*

150. Get hypnotized

151. Pose with a figure at a wax museum*

152. Attend a Cirque du Soleil show*

153. See a Vegas show*

154. Charter a yacht*

155. Hole number sixteen at Phoenix Open*

156. Get a tattoo*

157. Be present at a birth*

158. Build a house with Habitat for Humanity

159. Donate one thousand books*

160. Learn and play curling*

161. Stand-up paddleboard*

162. Bikram hot yoga class

163. Drive a snowmobile

164. Fly in a blimp

165. Sleep in an ice hotel

166. Visit a ghost town*

167. Helicopter into the Grand Canyon*

168. Dance at carnival in Rio de Janeiro

169. Drink Guinness in Dublin*

170. Drink red wine in Chile*

171. Do a Polar Bear Plunge

172. Zipline*

173. Cross Abbey Road Crossing—London

174. See the Mona Lisa—Paris*

175. Visit beaches at Normandy—France*

176. Visit redwood forest*

177. Air Combat USA*

178. Attend World Series

179. Attend Mardi Gras—New Orleans*

180. Visit Prague

181. Visit Kuala Lumpur—Malaysia*

182. Visit Hong Kong

183. Visit Shanghai*

184. Ride ATVs*

185. Certified for sailboating*

186. Swim with stingrays*

187. Camel ride on Broome Beach—Australia*

188. Relax in a natural hot spring*

189. Ride horse and carriage*

190. See the salmon run

191. Shear a sheep

192. Win age group—triathlon 70.3*

193. Win Ironman age group

194. Win age group—Olympic triathlon*

195. Qualify and compete in USA Triathlon Nationals*

196. Compete as member of Team USA in World Long Course Tri*

197. 365 photo challenge book*

198. Cross the Panama Canal*

199. Do an Everglades tour*

200. Visit Bhutan

201. Be recognized worldwide as authority in my field*

202. Arrive by seaplane*

203. Kayak the Chicago River*

204. Climb a glacier*

205. Visit Antarctica*

206. Visit Patagonia—Chile*

207. Bike Big Sur

208. Attend a presidential inauguration

209. Deliver a TED Talk

210. Attend a Bat Mitzvah*

211. Attend Super Bowl*

212. Attend Final Four*

213. Fourth of July in DC*

214. Ride a double-decker bus in London*

215. Carry the Olympic torch

216. Finish a corn maze

217. Fly in a private jet*

218. Go indoor skydiving*

219. Mush a dogsled*

220. Marathon at North Pole*

221. Play bocce ball*

222. Push a stone at Stonehenge

223. Read fifty-two books in one year

224. Ride a helicopter*

225. See Old Faithful in Yellowstone

226. Tour Acropolis in Greece*

227. Sleep in a rainforest*

228. Overnight in a treehouse*

229. Speak in a foreign country with a translator*

230. Stand on the equator*

231. Visit Anne Frank's house—Amsterdam

232. Write a children's book

233. Climb a rock wall*

234. Win age group—marathon*

235. Swim with a dolphin*

236. Night snorkel with manta rays*

237. Drive across USA coast to coast*

238. Visit a concentration camp*

239. Experience weightlessness—zero gravity

240. Visit active volcano*

241. Run with bulls in Pamplona

242. See Mount Rushmore*

243. Eat a meal from world-class chef*

244. Ride a gondola in Venice*

245. Learn to surf*

246. Visit the Hoover Dam

247. Hike Rim2Rim Grand Canyon*

248. Visit Christ the Redeemer Statue*

249. Walk Colosseum in Rome*

250. Visit Machu Picchu via Inca Trail*

251. Visit Jerusalem*

252. Give a commencement speech

253. Fly an airplane*

254. Eat at a Brazilian steakhouse, in Brazil*

255. Visit the Louvre—Paris*

256. Visit Saint Mark's Basilica—Venice*

257. Visit Dubrovnik in Croatia*

258. Edge walk the tower in Auckland, New Zealand*

259. Watch baseball game at Wrigley Field*

260. Set up passive income streams*

261. Ride a Segway*

262. Watch a Broadway play*

263. Visit Sistine Chapel*

264. Ride London Eye*

265. Visit Victoria Falls

266. Visit Sydney Opera House*

267. Walk Golden Gate Bridge*

268. Visit Grand Tetons / American safari*

269. Crater Lake Rim Runs Oregon—Register Jan 1

270. Catalina Island Eco Marathon—Early Nov

271. Go to Duke basketball camp

272. Visit/tour Cia*

273. Air Force One

274. Ryder Cup*

275. Visit Pompeii*

276. Yankee Stadium*

277. Basketball Hall of Fame*

278. Fenway Park*

279. Wrigley Field*

280. Olympic Club Golf*

281. Horseback riding*

282. White-water rafting*

283. Sequoia National Park*

284. West Point*

285. Air Force Academy*

286. Navy SEALs Coronado Tour*

287. Northern Lights*

288. Climb Wayna Picchu*

289. Climb Kilimanjaro

290. Chile wine country*

291. Royal Gorge Suspension Bridge*

292. Graceland

293. John Muir Trail in Yosemite

294. Potato Chip Rock San Diego*

295. Learn to play half a song on piano

296. Uganda Gorilla Safari

297. Diamond Head Summit*

298. Koko Crater Summit*

299. Cuba marathon*

300. Israel*

301. Vietnam*

302. Bali/Indonesia*

303. Pearl Harbor*

304. Velodrome*

305. Guatemala

306. Costa Rica

307. Amalfi Coast

308. Lisbon

309. Iceland

310. Sweden/Norway

311. Wrap a snake around my neck

312. Host a family reunion*

313. Kiss on top of a Ferris wheel

314. Receive a fan letter*

315. Share cab with stranger*

316. Blow glass

317. Refinish a piece of furniture*

318. Be on a radio show*

319. Bet at the dog races*

320. Dance on a bar*

321. Dance with Ellen DeGeneres

322. Go to movie by myself*

323. Be in the newspaper*

324. Ride a mechanical bull*

325. See a 3D movie*

326. See the Tour de France

327. Set a Guinness World Record*

328. Walk the red carpet

329. Get a mani/pedi*

330. Have a professional photo shoot*

331. Puerto Rico / San Juan*

332. Nepal/Katmandu*

333. Delhi/India*

334. Sri Lanka*

335. Attend *Price Is Right* show*

336. PGA Tourney*

337. Churchill War Room

338. Bangkok—float market and elephant ride*

339. Rim2Rim2Rim*

340. Jakarta*

341. Surabaya/Philippines*

342. Manila*

343. Vietnam Tunnels / Saigon*

344. Magic Castle*

345. Kenya*

346. Kayak downtown Chicago*

347. Havana, Cuba*

348. Rappelling a cliff*

349. Holy City / Western Wall*

350. Makhtesh erosion crater*

351. Hike Masada*

352. Dead Sea float / lowest place on earth*

353. Bethlehem*

354. World Holocaust Center / Jerusalem*

355. Witness wild beast migration*

356. Have palm read

357. Fly in private jet*

358. Eat insect*

359. Stomp grapes*

360. Be asked for autograph*

361. Be on jumbotron on stadium*

362. Get a standing ovation*

363. Saber a champagne bottle

364. Walk on nude beach … naked

365. Axe throwing*

366. Ride an elephant*

367. Ride in a tuk tuk*

368. Sleep in overnight train*

369. Book on Times Square*

370. Drink at Guinness Brewery*

371. Hear Andrea Bocelli sing

372. Van Gogh Museum*

373. Run marathon with grandkids

374. Antelope Canyon, Arizona

375. Badlands National Park, South Dakota

376. The Quiraing / Skye, Scotland

377. Canyon de Chelly, Arizona

378. Easter Island, Chile

379. Museum Island, Berlin

380. The Alhambra, Granada, Spain

381. Cinque Terre, Mediterranean, Italy

382. Abu Simbel, Egypt

383. Doha, Qatar

384. Terracotta Warriors, China

385. Golden Temple Dambulla, Sri Lanka

386. Bagan, Myanmar, Burma

387. San Juan Islands, Washington

388. Maritime Provinces, Canada

389. Biscayne National Park, Florida

390. Bora Bora, French Polynesia

As of 7/10/2021, 293/390 done or 75 percent.

Earlier, I discussed some of my most memorable bucket list experiences. I've shared several more here for those interested in hearing more.

1. Marathon all seven continents: I expected Antarctica to be my favorite on this journey, but the minimal snow at the time and the repetitiveness of running a short route bumped it down a notch. Poetic that my final continent marathon would be on the Great Wall of China. The route and overall experience was a once-in-a-lifetime experience for sure, and extra special was lifelong friend Rick Iovine participating. Since the snow was sparse in Antarctica, good friend Mark Moses and I elected to head north to the polar circle for a marathon, where we got all we were asking for and then some! This marathon ranks as my all-time-favorite marathon.

2. Ironman World Championship in Hawaii: While Ironman is the same distance in all races (140.6 miles of swim/bike/run), whenever speaking with people familiar with the topic, the question always asked is "Have you done Hawaii?" Knocking

this off the list with so many great friends and family was a life highlight. Of special note is that my wife, Bonnie, was always my biggest cheerleader, and she was present at every one of the fifteen Ironmans I completed.

3. North Pole Marathon: Of the ninety-five marathons run, my favorite is this one. Below zero temps, held in Greenland on the polar circle, snow to knees for first 10K, ice based for the 26.2 miles, and a point-to-point route brought so much beauty during such an epic day. I was once again joined by my buddy Mark Moses, and we extended our stay and toured this remarkable country.

4. Presidential libraries: Thirteen libraries visited over a ten-year period, with lots of leadership learning along the way, as was detailed in an earlier chapter. It was fun to race my friend and book publisher Adam Witty to see who would finish first. I narrowly beat him, as he fell one short with, of all things, the library I grabbed first—Bill Clinton.

5. Great Wall Marathon: The Great Wall of China is worth a visit in its own right, but to race a marathon on it is taking it to another level. Add to that it was my final continent in my quest for marathons on all seven continents, and it becomes a bucket list highlight. Close friend Rick Iovine joined me again, and we both agreed this was one of our very best outings.

6. Acropolis in Athens: Bonnie and I teamed this visit up with our first Mediterranean cruise, visiting several Greek Isles and finishing up in Istanbul. The entire experience is forever in my memory, and the touring of the historic area of Athens was everything that I had imagined and more.

7. Mediterranean cruise: Bonnie and I became big fans of the Med and cruising and experienced four different outings, each with unique ports and memories. Venice, Rome, Barcelona, Santorini, Istanbul, and Dubrovnik are just a few of the highlight stops.

8. Moscow and St. Petersburg: Ever since high school, Red Square and Moscow have always held out a fascination for me. What a treat that my speaking business would take me not once but twice to Moscow. The Kremlin and Red Square were all that I had imagined; however, the rest of the city was nothing to necessarily get excited about—more of a large, crowded city that could be seen anywhere. The jewel of the visit was a visit to St. Petersburg, and we were blessed with ideal tourist weather. In the interest of simplicity, I would describe it as a city similar to Paris, where buildings are works of art themselves and then are full of amazing world-renowned art as well.

9. Rome/Vatican: I've had the good fortune to visit this amazing city on several occasions, and each time it's with a sense of marvel and history. As Arnold is famous for saying, "I'll be back."

10. France/Paris: Museums, palaces, food, and beauty all wrapped together in the city of Paris. Long on the bucket list for both my wife, Bonnie, and me, we reveled in our visit, albeit too short. When I lost Bonnie to pancreatic cancer, I figured I would ride the rest of life out as a single guy. That all changed when I met my soul mate, Karen Caplan, a favored client for over twenty years. I'm committed to now return with Karen to draw in this city's magic.

11. Budapest: We arrived by way of a river cruise on the Danube, and the grandeur of this capital city of Hungary was profound. One of the most photogenic cities in Europe, with the majestic riverside Parliament Building and the stunning basilicas, the city begs for a longer visit than what's afforded on a cruise.

12. Cover of magazine: Here was yet another stretch. I had been published in many magazines worldwide, which was gratifying in itself. But somehow making the cover had eluded me. In fact, I decided to publish my own magazine (*Get Jack'd*) so I would make the cover each issue! Finally, a couple of years later, I legitimately made it with *Culturama*, based in India. Truly a treat! Special thanks to editor Rohini Manian for the invitation and to EO for inviting me to speak throughout India.

13. Bungee jump: The Kawarau Gorge Suspension Bridge was the first-ever bungee jump, and the river water sure comes up quick for your submersion! Later in the day, I headed to the Nevis Canyon bungee, at the time the highest bungee in the world at 134 meters above the canyon. Not for the faint of heart, it was a full eight-second drop before snatched. Thrill of a lifetime! And yes, I would do it again!

14. NCAA basketball finals: Best friend Rick Iovine and I have been lifelong college basketball fanatics, and our wives were not far behind in enthusiasm for the game, and in 2015 we got to knock this bucket list item off. Ever since the legendary John Wooden championship run at UCLA, I've viewed Coach Mike Krzyzewski in a similar vein at Duke. It was pure joy to be there to see Duke prevail over Wisconsin 68–63 in Indianapolis.

15. Team USA: I was out on a bike training ride and saw a rider with Team USA gear on. We had a good chat, and I learned that in the triathlon world, there was a Long Distance World Championship among countries, and it was possible for a guy my age to make the team. Right then, it went on the bucket list. In October 2011, my sister Valerie and I raced in the Myrtle Beach 70.3 Triathlon, and we both won spots on the team that day. Disappointingly, I caught the flu in Vitoria, Spain, and missed out on competing that day of the championship. Nonetheless, I take pride in making the team!

MARATHONS

Year	Number of Marathons	Number of States	States Total	Total Overall
1994	1	1	1	1
1995	1	1	2	2
1996	1	0	2	3
1997	0	0	2	3
1998	2	0	2	5
1999	0	0	2	5
2000	0	0	2	5
2001	0	0	2	5
2002	2	0	2	7
2003	2	0	2	9
2004	5	4	6	14
2005	5	5	11	19
2006	7	7	18	26
2007	5	4	22	31
2008	6	2	24	37
2009	2	2	26	39

2010	5	1	27	44
2011	6	3	30	50
2012	7	0	30	57
2013	5	5	35	62
2014	6	3	38	68
2015	11	6	44	79
2016	9	6	50	88
2017	2	0	50	90
2018	3	1	51	93
2019	2	0	51	95

NOTES:

1. It took twenty-four years from start to finish of the fifty states.

2. It shows fifty-one, as it's fifty states plus DC.

3. The fifty states went on my bucket list as a goal in 2004, when racing the Los Angeles Marathon—someone passed me with a shirt that said "I've run a marathon in all fifty states." When I asked about it, I learned there was an online club, and on it went to the bucket list. As such, the quest actually took me fourteen years once set as a goal.

4. One hundred marathons went on the bucket list in 2011, when I realized I had fifty completed, so why not! Expected completion in 2021, which would entail ten years once goal was set. From first marathon, twenty-seven years.

CONTINENTS

1. North America: #1—10/2/94—Portland, Oregon

2. Ironman UK: #29—8/19/07—Lake Sherborne

3. Ironman Australia: #35—4/6/08—Port Macquarie

4. Ironman Brazil: #42—5/30/10—Florianópolis

5. Ironman South Africa: #46—4/10/11—Port Elizabeth

6. Antarctica: #70—2/19/15

7. Great Wall of China: #92—5/19/18—Beijing

The journey covers a span of twenty-four years. The goal was set on the bucket list in 2008 and completed in 2018, taking ten years once goal was established.

MARATHON HISTORY

Date	State Number	City, State	Time
10-2-94	1	Portland, Oregon	4:28:22
1-21-95	2	San Diego, California	3:58:58
7-14-96	n/a	San Francisco, California	4:14:24
3-29-98	n/a	Los Angeles, California	5:14:23
6-21-98	n/a	San Diego RnR, California	4:42:21
3-03-02	n/a	Los Angeles, California	5:20:48
6-02-02	n/a	San Diego RnR, California	4:59:33
1-19-03	n/a	San Diego, California	5:56:44
3-2-03	n/a	Los Angeles, California	5:09:04

3-7-04	n/a	Los Angeles, California	5:11:00
4-17-04	3	Charlottesville, Virginia	5:04:00
5-30-04	4	Coeur d'Alene, Idaho	4:45:00
10-10-04	5	Chicago, Illinois	4:58:50
11-28-04	6	Seattle, Washington	4:46:00
1-9-05	7	Phoenix RnR, Arizona	4:52:00
1-30-05	8	Las Vegas, Nevada	5:22:00
5-1-05	9	Cincinnati, Ohio	5:11:33
10-1-05	10	Bristol, New Hampshire	5:25:00
11-20-05	11	Philadelphia, Pennsylvania	5:15:34
1-8-06	12	Disney World, Florida	5:23:52
3-5-06	13	Little Rock, Arkansas	5:04:35
4-29-06	14	Nashville, Tennessee	5:12:30
5-21-06	15	Wilmington, Delaware	5:02:06
10-29-06	16	Marine Corps, DC	5:21:33
11-5-06	17	New York City, New York	5:12:45
12-10-06	18	Dallas, Texas	5:09:00
4-16-07	19	Boston, Massachusetts	4:42:01
4-28-07	20	Louisville, Kentucky	4:45:00
8-19-07	n/a	Ironman UK	5:33:38
10-7-07	21	Minneapolis, Minnesota	4:58:38
10-13-07	22	Baltimore, Maryland	4:51:29
1-13-08	n/a	Disney World Goofy	5:36:00

2-16-08	23	Myrtle Beach, South Carolina	5:12:00
5-18-08	24	Green Bay, Wisconsin	4:56:00
4-6-08	n/a	Ironman Australia	5:50:34
4-21-08	n/a	Boston, Massachusetts	5:12:44
8-24-08	n/a	Ironman Canada	5:25:00
2-1-09	25	Mardi Gras, New Orleans, LA	5:25:16
9-19-09	26	Top of Utah, Utah	4:36:00
2-7-10	n/a	Surf City, California	4:50:00
4-17-10	n/a	Charlottesville, Virginia	4:57:41
5-30-10	n/a	Ironman Brazil	5:10:00
8-22-10	27	Pikes Peak, Colorado	10:30:00
11-28-10	n/a	Ironman Cozumel	5:15:00
3-5-11	n/a	Ironman New Zealand	4:51:14
4-10-11	n/a	Ironman South Africa	5:14:00
5-1-11	28	Providence, Rhode Island	3:56:59

Note: Boston Qualified!

6-18-11	29	Anchorage, Alaska	4:36:00
10-13-11	30	St. Louis, Missouri	4:20:00
12-04-11	n/a	Las Vegas, Nevada	4:40:00
2-05-12	n/a	Surf City, California	4:38:00
3-25-12	n/a	Ironman Melbourne, Australia	5:44:00
4-16-12	n/a	Boston, Massachusetts	5:50:00
5-16-12	n/a	Orange County, California	4:40:00

8-19-12	n/a	Ironman Mount Tremblant	5:37:34
10-7-12	n/a	Long Beach, California	4:39:00
11-18-12	n/a	Ironman Arizona	5:16:31
6-22-13	31	Charlevoix, Michigan	5:11:00
7-13-13	32	Grandfather Mountain, NC	5:15:00
8-17-13	33	Green River, Wyoming	5:50:00
10-12-13	34	Kona, Hawaii	6:48:57
11-2-13	35	Indianapolis, Indiana	4:58:47
2-16-14	36	Birmingham, Alabama	5:05:00
3-23-14	n/a	Ironman Cabo San Lucas	6:15:00
4-12-14	37	Abilene, Kansas	5:25:00
6-8-14	n/a	Ironman Cairns, Australia	5:58:00
10-11-14	38	Hartford, Connecticut	5:15:00
11-2-14	n/a	New York City, New York	5:32:00
2-1-15	n/a	Surf City, California	5:12:09
2-19-15	n/a	Antarctica	6:15:00
4-20-15	n/a	Boston, Massachusetts	5:07:00
5-10-15	39	Maine	5:34:00
5-17-15	40	Vermont	5:25:00
6-27-15	41	Iowa	5:10:00
8-16-15	n/a	Pikes Peak, Colorado	9:45:00
9-20-15	42	Omaha, Nebraska	5:08:00
10-10-15	43	West Virginia	5:04:00

11-22-15	n/a	Philadelphia, Pennsylvania	5:04:00
12-13-15	44	Tulsa, Oklahoma	6:58:00
2-7-16	n/a	Surf City, California	5:26:00
2-13-16	45	Mississippi	5:45:00
3-20-16	46	Georgia	5:45:00
5-1-16	n/a	OC, California	5:50:00
5-21-16	47	Fargo, North Dakota	5:50:00
7-10-16	48	Missoula, Montana	5:25:00
9-03-16	49	Roswell, New Mexico	5:41:00
10-9-16	50	South Dakota	5:30:00
10-29-16	n/a	Polar Circle Greenland	6:42:00
2-5-17	n/a	Surf City, California (Adam/Mel)	6:07:00
11-5-17	n/a	New York City (For Bon)	6:25:00
4-22-18	51	Ocean Drive, New Jersey	5:41:00
5-19-18	n/a	Great Wall of China	7:47:00
11-4-18	n/a	New York City, New York	5:40:00
2-3-19	n/a	Surf City, California	5:33:00
11-10-19	n/a	Havana, Cuba	5:55:00

TRIATHLONS AND IRONMANS

Year	Sprint	Olympic	70.3	Ironman	Life Total	DNF
2004	1	0	0	0	1	0
2005	0	0	1	0	2	0
2006	1	1	0	0	4	2
2007	0	2	3	1	10	0
2008	0	5	1	2	18	0
2009	1	3	1	1	24	0
2010	0	2	2	2	30	0
2011	0	1	3	2	36	0
2012	0	0	2	4	42	0
2013	0	0	3	1	46	0
2014	0	4	0	2	52	1
2015	0	1	1	0	54	0
2016	0	1	1	0	56	0

NOTES:

1. Ironman goes on bucket list in 1982, as a result of Julie Moss crawl over finish line in Kona. From 1982 to 2007, it takes twenty-five years to complete first Ironman.

2. In 2008, put Kona Ironman World Championship on bucket list; raced it in 2013, five years later.

3. In 2005, put 70.3 World Championship on bucket list; completed it in 2007, two years later.

4. In 2008, put *Ironman—all continents except Antarctica* on bucket list; completed it in 2011, three years later.

5. Several podium finishes along the way.

6. Overall summary: three sprints; twenty Olympics; seventeen 70.3s; fifteen 140.6s; three DNFs.

TRIATHLON HISTORY

Date	Race	Swim T1	Bike T2	Run	Total
3-14-04	Temecula	4:54	56:16	27:55	1:31:47
	Sprint	150 yards	16 miles	5K	
6-13-05	Honu	1:02:51	3:51:58	3:05:11	8:11:00
	70.3	1.2 miles	56 miles	13.1 miles	
4-02-06	Temecula	6:08	58:14	27:08	1:31:33
	Sprint	150 yards	16 miles	5K	
4-22-06	Desert	23:44 4:32	1:11:00 1:41	53:12	2:33:54
	International	.9 miles	25 miles	10K	
6-01-06	Honu	1:15	DNF		
7-29-06	Vineman	70.3	DNF		
3-28-07	Mooloolaba	31:40	1:27:00	1:02:58	3:01:40
	International	.9 miles	25 miles	10K	
6-02-07	Honu	43:03 5:11	3:11:00 2:51	2:26:00	6:28:55
	70.3	1.2 miles	56 miles	13.1 miles	

7-21-07	Vineman 70.3	59:56 1.2 miles	3:35:00 56 miles	2:40:00 13.1 miles	7:19:44
8-19-07	Ironman UK 140.6	1:22:39 10:11 2.4 miles	7:38:59 6:15 112 miles	5:33:38 26.2 miles	14:51:18
9-06-07	LA Tri Olympic	36:42 6:21 .9 miles	1:18:26 3:54 25 miles	1:01:01 10K	3:06:02
11-10-07	Clearwater World 70.3	43:34 1.2 miles	2:55:56 56 miles	2:25:16 13.1 miles	6:14:19
3-27-08	Mooloolaba International	35:07 .9 miles	1:25:28 25 miles	58:18 10K	2:58:53
4-6-08	Australia Ironman 140.6	1:29:10 2.4 miles	7:24:22 112 miles	5:50:34 26.2 miles	14:44:07
5-31-08	Honu 70.3	46:09 6:09 1.2 miles	3:16:00 3:30 56 miles	2:31:00 13.1 miles	6:43:34
6-29-08	San Diego International	17:33 4:03 1K	57:27 2:16 30K	57:34 10K	2:18:51
8-9-08	Pendleton International	12:48 1.5K	1:00:09 40K	26:17 5K	1:39:00
8-24-08	Canada Ironman 140.6	1:28:00 5:00 2.4 miles	7:19:00 4:00 112 miles	5:25:00 26.2 miles	14:22:33
9-07-08	LA Tri Olympic	33:21 3:53 .9 miles	1:19:54 3:00 25 miles	57:45 10K	2:57:55
9-28-08	OC Mission Viejo Olympic	32:59 1 mile	1:24:00 25 miles	1:05:00 10K	3:09:31
03-28-09	Mooloolaba International	35:56 6:28 .9 miles	1:26:00 2:03 25 miles	58:45 10K	3:10:00
06-28-09	Philly Olympic	29:24 4:37 .9 miles	1:24:46 2:53 25 miles	58:09 10K	2:59:51

07-12-09	Carlsbad Sprint	20:00 1K	50:00 25K	26:00 5K	1:36
09-13-09	DC Olympic	32:00 1 mile	1:15:00 25 miles	60:00 10K	2:58
10-25-09	Austin 70.3	41:58:31	3:05:34	2:15:26	6:12:34
11-22-09	Ironman Arizona 2.4 miles	1:26:44 9:07 112 miles	6:53:01 5:03 26.2 miles	5:50:00	14:24:40
03-27-10	Oceanside 70.3	41:19	3:06:54	2:27:33	6:25:06
04-11-10	Frogman 70.3	1:04:00	3:10:00	2:43:00	6:57:00
05-30-10	Ironman Brazil	1:18:28 4:46	6:31:13 7:08	5:09:00	13:10:55
06-27-10	Philly Olympic	27:00	1:20:00	57:00	2:56:00
08-29-10	Chicago Olympic	30:00	1:15:00	1:10:00	3:09:00
11-28-10	Ironman Cozumel	1:29:00	7:03:00	5:15:00	14:00:00
03-05-11	Ironman New Zealand	1:23:52	7:00:01	4:51:14	13:35:06
04-10-11	Ironman South Africa	1:26:00	6:26:00	5:14:00	13:19:00

Note: Podium finish—third in age group.

06-04-11	Honu 70.3	44:09	3:04:00	2:16:00	6:14:25
06-26-11	Philly Olympic	30:00	1:20:00	53:00	2:53:00
09-25-11	Orangeman 70.3	47:44	3:29:00	2:31:00	6:47:00
10-08-11	Myrtle Beach 70.3	49:00	3:00:00	2:05:00	6:01:00
03-04-12	Ironman New Zealand (70.3 Alt)	52:47	3:08:00	2:10:00	6:25:49
03-25-12	Ironman Melbourne, Australia	1:41:52	6:17:54	5:44:18	13:56:45

**** Thirty-eight triathlons to date, beginning 3/14/04****

242

06-02-12	Honu 70.3	47:00	3:12:00	2:20:00	6:32:00
08-19-12	Mount Tremblant Ironman	1:30:00	6:30:00	5:37:34	13:54:41
10-14-12	Magic Mountain	42:16	4:36:55	3:01:33	8:31:28
11-18-12	Ironman Tempe, Arizona	1:32:00	6:05:00	5:16:31	13:06:09
5-04-13	St. George, Utah, 70.3	49.10	3:32:00	3:05:00	7:39:13
6-01-13	Honu 70.3	48:07	3:18:59	2:57:30	7:15:44
9-15-13	Moo 70.3	49:00	3:13:00	2:38:00	6:52:28
10-12-13	Kona	1:47:32	7:12:08	6:48:57	16:05:11
3-23-14	Cabo	1:30:00	7:29:00	6:15:00	15:41:30
6-8-14	Cairns, Australia	1:38:00	7:05:00	5:59:00	14:58:00
6-29-14	Challenge Atlantic City	2:20:00	6:47:00	2:20:00	DNF
8-3-14	NYC Olympic	16:53	1:23:59	55:19	2:49:43
8-23-14	Santa Barb Triathlon	38:00	2:05:00	1:40:00	4:30:00
9-21-14	South Dakota Olympic	47:00	1:10:00	56:00	3:01:37
10-26-14	Oceanside Olympic	33:00	1:19:00	57:00	2:55:00
7-19-15	NYC Olympic	24:00	1:26:00	1:02:00	3:02:35
9-13-15	Cedar Point 70.3	58:00	3:18:00	2:15:00	6:43:32
6-04-16	Honu 70.3	50:00	3:34:00	3:14:00	7:52:37
8-13-16	National USA Olympic	45:41	1:26:55	1:05:29	3:25:00

Fifty-seven triathlons completed through Dec 31, 2016, beginning March 2004.

APPENDIX 7: GOLF

Top 100 Playable Golf Courses in the United States

Order	Course	State	Date	Score
1	The Lodge at Ventana Canyon	AZ	2-27-2000	87
2	The Links at Spanish Bay	CA	7-9-2000	99
3	Pebble Beach	CA	7-9-2000	95
4	Spyglass Hill	CA	7-10-2000	92
5	Troon North—Monument	AZ	7-19-2000	96
6	Laquinta—Mountain	CA	7-29-2000	96
7	Pelican Hill—North	CA	9-2-2000	96
8	Kapalua—Plantation	HI	9-12-2000	84
9	Princeville—Prince	HI	9-14-2000	91
10	Kauai Lagoons—Kiele	HI	9-16-2000	87
11	Troon North—Pinnacle	AZ	10-25-2000	91
12	The Boulders—South	AZ	10-25-2000	89
13	Grand Cypress—New Course	FL	12-9-2000	90
14	Pelican Hill—South	CA	1-21-2001	90
15	Four Seasons—Aviara	CA	2-19-2001	88
16	Emerald Dunes	SC	3-3-2001	86

17	Primm Valley—Lakes	NV	3-17-2001	96
18	Nemacolin Woodlands—Mystic Rock	PA	4-1-2001	86
19	Torrey Pines—South	CA	5-29-2001	93
20	Legend Trail	AZ	6-29-2001	89
21	Grayhawk—Raptor	AZ	6-30-2001	101
22	The Westin—Innisbrook	FL	7-29-2001	89
23	The Challenge at Manele	HI	10-8-2001	87
24	The Koolau	HI	10-12-2001	88
25	Fowler's Mill	OH	6-16-2002	83
26	Treetops Sylvan—Rick Smith	MI	7-11-2002	91
27	Treetops Sylvan—Tom Fazio	MI	7-11-2002	91
28	Bay Harbor	MI	7-12-2002	88
29	Boyne Highlands—Heather	MI	7-13-2002	95
30	Pasatiempo	CA	9-13-2002	91
31	The Raven—Sabino Springs	AZ	11-24-2002	91
32	World Woods—Rolling Oaks	FL	2-2-2003	97
33	World Woods—Pine Barrens	FL	2-2-2003	91
34	PGA West—TPC Stadium	CA	2-24-2003	96
35	Shadow Creek	NV	4-28-2003	92
36	Wolf Creek	NV	4-27-2003	93
37	Pacific Dunes	OR	5-17-2003	85
38	Bandon Dunes	OR	5-18-2003	91
39	Mauna Lani—North	HI	7-4-2003	90

40	Mauna Kea—Beach	HI	7-6-2003	94
41	Tullymore	MI	7-23-2003	84
42	Pilgrim's Run	MI	7-24-2003	85
43	High Pointe	MI	7-28-2003	92
44	Coeur D'Alene	ID	5-29-2004	83
45	Beechtree	MD	7-11-2004	87
46	Bulle Rock	MD	7-11-2004	96
47	Blue Heron	NJ	7-16-2004	91
48	Cog Hill—#4	IL	8-2-2004	93
49	Kemper Lakes	IL	8-3-2004	85
50	Castle Pines North	CO	8-15-2004	93
51	Pine Hill	NJ	8-27-2004	92
52	Cantigny—Woodside/Lakeside	IL	10-8-2004	87
53	The Glen Club	IL	10-9-2004	85
54	We-Ko-Pa	AZ	1-7-2005	84
55	Grayhawk (Talon)	AZ	1-8-2005	91
56	The Experience at Keole	HI	3-1-2005	84
57	Longaberger	OH	4-29-2005	89
58	Talking Stick (North)	AZ	5-16-2005	79
59	Edgewood Tahoe	NV	6-24-2005	86
60	Lost Canyons (Sky)	CA	8-12-2005	91
61	Whistling Straits	WI	9-5-2005	97
62	Whistling Straits (Irish)	WI	9-5-2005	94

63	Blackwolf Run—River	WI	9-6-2005	102
64	Blackwolf Run—Meadow Valley	WI	9-6-2005	96
65	The Wilds	MN	9-13-2005	85
66	Deacon's Lodge	MN	9-14-2005	88
67	La Purisma	CA	11-15-2005	87
68	Bay Hill	FL	1-7-2006	90
69	Reflection Bay	NV	1-10-2006	89
70	The Judge	AL	4-27-2006	94
71	Lighthouse Sound	MD	5-19-2006	88
72	The General	IL	6-11-2006	88
73	University Ridge	WI	6-12-2006	90
74	Bandon Trails	OR	1-20-2007	91
75	Rustic Canyon	CA	2-9-2007	89
76	Pinehurst No. 2	NC	3-1-2007	93
77	The Dunes	SC	2-17-2008	88
78	Hapuna	HI	6-1-2008	84
79	Hualalai	HI	6-3-2008	80
80	Trump National LA	CA	8-11-2008	94
81	The Bear	MI	6-21-2013	94
82	Tobacco Road	NC	7-14-2013	84
83	Old Macdonald	OR	8-4-2013	101
84	Atlantic City Country Club	NJ	7-21-2014	91
85	Bethpage Black	NY	8-1-2014	93

86	Trump National Doral	FL	3-19-2015	97
87	Brickyard Crossing	IN	4-6-2015	96
88	Streamsong Red	FL	12-5-2015	90
89	Streamsong Blue	FL	12-6-2015	98
90	Cascata	NV	1-16-2016	98
91	Prairie Club Dunes	NE	8-15-2016	93
92	Prairie Club Pines	NE	8-16-2016	101
93	Wynn Golf Club	NV	7-17-2017	90
94	Spring Creek	VA	4-5-2018	88
95	Pine Valley	NJ	6-5-2018	102

Here are a few of my favorite golf experiences, listed in the order in which played.

1. Ventana Canyon, Mountain Course: February 27, 2000. I was in Arizona for a speaking gig and snuck this in the day before my gig. Beautiful resort at the Lodge in Arizona, and the course was impeccably groomed and fairly designed. This was a great course to start the journey, and a score of eighty-seven made it all the sweeter. My only complaint was being out there without friends to share the experience, but it was a solid reminder that this would be the case with several if I were to have a shot at completing one hundred.

2. The Links at Spanish Bay: July 9, 2000. A golf vacation weekend at one of the prized golf destinations, with great friends and spouses—doesn't get much better than that! While I had previously played all three of these world-class courses, in order to qualify for the Top 100 bucket list, they

had to be replayed beginning in the year 2000. Rick Iovine came out from the East Coast and joined in on the fun with Mark Moses and Pete MacDonald rounding out the foursome. Not only is the Monterey, California, area a mecca for golf, but it is packed with world-class culinary and art experiences. As such, our spouses joined us in those pursuits as we made our way around the links. Two rounds played this day, here in the morning and Pebble Beach in the afternoon. Course conditions and layout were superb, but the winds can play havoc with your ball flight. I fell victim to those winds, carding a fat ninety-nine. The highlight was Pete holing out a 170-yard shot for an eagle on number nine. A favorite here is making it back for the sunset bagpipe player, as we toasted all of us with great wine over the firepit adjacent to the course.

3. Pebble Beach: July 9, 2000. I fared better here, carding a ninety-five. While playing this tract is always special, in my opinion there are seven extraordinary golf holes here, while the other eleven are merely so-so. Those extraordinary holes of six, seven, eight, nine, ten, fourteen, and eighteen more than make up for the rest. Best advice I can ever give is to be sure to walk this beauty and take a caddie. This course deserves that special treatment. I've never made it through a round here without taking several photos!

4. Spyglass Hill: July 10, 2000. Same group of friends on this amazing tract. When I finished playing it, I went into the pro shop and had them custom embroider a hat that said, "This is where God lives." The course opens with a par five, with a long shot from the tee box. The first five holes work their way with ocean views; then the course heads back into a more

"tree'd" experience. Another description might be *tight*. Of the three courses played this weekend with good friends, this was my favorite and continues to be through today. Bonus was my score of ninety-two.

5. Kapalua Plantation: September 12, 2000. I just now skipped several terrific courses, which was bound to happen when trying to highlight a few from a list of the Top 100. This is one of my all-time-favorite courses, always in impeccable condition and with unending views. While the course has real teeth in terms of difficulty, there is enough room with resort-style fairways to generally keep the ball on the short hairs. I was beyond thrilled with my eighty-four, including a front nine four over par! One of my favorites is to bring friends out for their first round here and see their facial expressions for holes seventeen and eighteen. Priceless.

6. The Prince Course: September 12, 2000. Justifiably rated as the number one course in the state of Hawaii. Be careful in picking the time of year because this side of Kauai can be rain soaked. This Robert Trent Jones–designed course will bring all the challenges a golfer could ever want and then some! While I had played this one prior to working on the Top 100 list, this time I was better prepared for the beast and happily recorded my ninety-one. Simply stated, not to be missed.

7. The Challenge at Manele: October 8, 2001. This is truly a beauty on the little island of Lanai off the coast of Maui in Hawaii. This Jack Nicklaus–designed course is a target-style desert links layout, while every hole provides an expansive view of the brilliant blue sea. Volcanic slopes, lava rock formations, and mesmerizing scenery all come into play. The

front nine is a mere "warm-up" for what's to come on the back. While hole twelve is the signature hole and deservedly so, the seventeenth probably requires Hawaii's most demanding shot. I felt good with my eighty-eight and played several times during my stay at the resort. On subsequent trips to Maui, I always squeeze in a ferry ride over to Lanai to once again tee it up.

8. Koolau: October 12, 2001. For many golfers, this would not make the highlights section, but it for sure is a personal favorite of mine. At the time I played it (and have been back several more times since then), it was ranked as the hardest course in the United States. Back tee slope was 162, and the white tee box was even rated 132 over 6,406. Hole eighteen is rated as the hardest hole on the course, and the tee box has a sign stating, "You are about to play the hardest hole on the hardest course in the United States." However, playing those shorter tees will allow the golfer to skip many of the two hundred–plus carries over barrancas from the tees. This monster is carved out of a rainforest some fifteen miles outside of Honolulu, often referred to as *King Kong in a skirt*! The pro shop recommendation is to bring at a minimum the number of balls equivalent to your handicap/index. A successful day is any when you finish and do not lose all those. As such I was pretty happy with my eighty-eight, losing four balls for the day. Bring your camera and a buddy; it's like playing in Jurassic Park.

9. Bay Harbor Golf Club: July 12, 2002. Based in Boyne, Michigan, and home to several Top 100 courses, this twenty-seven-hole beauty premiered on the list at number eight! I

was fortunate to play all three nines, and each are uniquely different from the others. The combo of the links and quarry nines are what brought the course to fame, but for sure don't overlook the preserve nine. The links is incredibly scenic, very reminiscent of Hawaii courses, while overlooking Little Traverse Bay. It is sometimes referred to as the "Pebble Beach of the Midwest." Once you have played it, you will have difficulty choosing which two nines for a replay. Happy with my eight-eight.

10. Pasatiempo: September 13, 2002. The only course on the Top 100 designed by the legendary Scottish designer Dr. Alister MacKenzie is an often-overlooked tract in Santa Cruz, just north of the Pebble Beach gang. If that name sounds familiar, think Cypress Point and Augusta National. Good friend Gerry Layo turned me on to this classic beauty, and we shared the round together on our way to "the Pebble Beach gang." In the year 2000 it was ranked number seventeen, and it's every bit of that!

11. PGA West TPC Stadium: February 24, 2003. Here is what the developers instructed architect Pete Dye: "Build us the hardest golf course in the world." This course more than any other is known for sending pros in the opposite direction and for good reason. Witness 250,000 gorse-like shrubs, eight lakes trimmed with rough-cut boulders, and deep and lengthy bunkers everywhere you look—just some of the distractions. Located near Palm Springs, my good friend and business partner Mark Moses joined me for a day in what we called the "house of pain." Bragging rights for me with a birdie on number two and a par on the legendary "Alcatraz" seventeenth.

12. Shadow Creek: April 28, 2003. Steve Wynn instructed legendary architect Pete Dye to build a "mature" golf course on a flat piece of desert just outside of Las Vegas. My partner Gerry Layo gifted me this experience, and what a gift, as at the time, a round of golf was a princely $1,000. On opening day Pete Dye addressed an audience to declare the course was open for play. In his remarks he indicated that Steve Wynn gave him an unlimited budget to build the course, and "he exceeded the budget." This course is a miracle project of perfection, including the clubhouse and practice area. In fact, each foursome is provided its own private tee boxes separate from any other groups. The course was not listed in the year 2000, as the fee was categorized as too expensive to be included in a list of *playable*. That was amended in 2002, as it was listed number seven, and if cameras were allowed, I suspect as many photos would have been shot as my ninety-two strokes. Gerry, a seven-index golfer, carded an eighty-four. The scorecard just didn't seem to matter, as the experience alone was enough to raise your heartbeat. Oh, and the yardage book was a coffee table-like photobook of 125 pages!

13. Wolf Creek: April 27, 2003. Opened in the year 2000, it premiered on the Top 100 in 2002 in position number forty-eight. This unique tract located about an hour and a half outside of Vegas in Mesquite, Nevada, is a definite golfer must. I've flown to Vegas from Southern California when golfer friends are due to visit Vegas just to see their faces on arrival at Wolf Creek. Gerry Layo and I tackled this one the day prior to Shadow Creek, making for one memorable golfing visit. Stunning white bunkers seem to be everywhere,

and the pristine fairways demand target golf. No matter what tee box level you choose, be sure to climb to the "tips" on number two and try to even guess your target landing area. By far this was the most visually dramatic golf course I have ever played.

14. Pacific Dunes: May 17, 2003. Located in Bend, Oregon, this is my favorite golf destination. A collection of world-class golf, with additional courses being added regularly. Gerry Layo and I arrived to play in a two-man best ball tourney. We led the tourney from start until the last day, where we went on to fold and finish "out of the money." Built in 2001, and in 2002 premiering on the Top 100 list in the number two spot, this was my favorite course in the world until 2018. The resort courses are pure links courses, walking only with literally hundreds of caddies to choose from. For me, Pacific Dunes is the ultimate golf experience sitting on the coast of Oregon. Winds that will haunt you well beyond the round, shore pines to sixty-foot sand dunes, and gorse seemingly everywhere, this is the proverbial man-versus-nature experience. Other than hole sixteen, I'd put any of the others up against most any golf holes out there. Consider this a must visit, including the practice area, which includes a one-acre putting green!

15. Bandon Dunes: May 18, 2003. Sister course to Pacific Dunes and ranked number nine in 2002, this is, as proclaimed, "golf as it was meant to be," with the spirit of Scotland's ancient links, with ocean views on nearly every hole. Many would argue this tract outdoes Pacific Dunes, and it would be hard to argue otherwise. *Golfweek* said it best: "Picture a cross

between Pebble Beach and Carnoustie—with a pinch of Pine Valley for good measure—and you have Bandon Dunes."

16. Coeur D'Alene: May 29, 2004. I played this beauty twice on Memorial Day weekend and squeezed in running a marathon in between in my quest for a marathon in all fifty states. Both days my front nine cards were in the thirties, only to blow up on the back, shooting eighty-three and eighty-five. You can certainly find tougher tracks but none more beautiful and impeccably maintained. Sure, other courses have their signature hole but none as unique and famous as number fourteen, par three, sporting the world's first and only moveable floating green! The green is repositioned daily and can be 100 yards one day and 175 the next. A boat ride from mainland to the green is the only way to get there, and special gifts are in store for pars, birdies, and aces. Not to be missed.

17. Bulle Rock: July 11, 2004. The second of two Top 100 courses played in one day in the state of Maryland. The overwhelming consensus of our foursome was this was one of the toughest courses we had ever played. Longtime friend Bruce Nosse, fellow entrepreneur friend Jim Kenefick, and brother-in-law Craig Nicholls posted scores of 101, 97, 103, and 96 to lend evidence to the statement. It is ranked by many as the number one must-play course in the state of Maryland; come prepared with "game." It was ranked number twenty-five on the 2002 list. We all left with great memories despite the high scores. My memory was best of all, as on the thirty-sixth hole of the day, I holed a sixty-foot putt for all the money!

18. Pine Hill: August 27, 2004. Ranked number thirty-one on the 2002 Top 100 list, this beast of a tract is located just two

miles from the world-legendary Pine Valley Golf Club. Named often as the most challenging course in New Jersey, it brought memories of my visit to Bulle Rock. The course was built atop a former ski slope, so flat lies are rare, and the thick woods and sharp drop-offs serve up plenty of opportunities for penalty shots to accumulate. Lifelong best friend Rick Iovine joined me for a fun day, Rick carding an eighty-seven and me a ninety-two.

19. We-Ko-Pa: January 7, 2005. I flew to Phoenix, Arizona, to knock down two Top 100s, followed by running my seventh state marathon in my quest of fifty states. Bonnie joined me for the weekend, which began on a bad foot with the airlines losing my golf clubs for a day. The club set me up with new shoes and a rental set, whereupon I fell in love with the Cleveland Launcher and added it to my permanent set. Club matched me up with two pros from Canada, and Bonnie joined in for a ride along. Ranked number thirty-eight on the 2004 list, it deserved its ranking. Great layout, no houses on the course, and gorgeous views. Playing alongside the pros sure helped my game—eighty-four for the day!

20. Edgewood Tahoe: June 24, 2005. My birthday treat to business partner Gerry Layo at one of my most favorite spots in the world—Lake Tahoe, Nevada. Ranked number sixty-nine on the year 2000 Top 100, the tree-lined fairways backdropped by snow-frosted mountains stretching along a bluer-than-blue alpine lake make for a feast for the eyes. This Fazio-designed beauty is impeccably manicured, and the closing holes alone are worth the price of admission. Only fitting on his birthday, Gerry took home a prized shirt from the gift shop, his eighty-one beating my eighty-six handily.

21. Whistling Straits: September 5, 2005. Ranked number eight on the 2002 Top 100 list, this course is an architectural wonder in Kohler, Wisconsin. Two foursomes of friends over two days, packing in this beauty along with three other Top 100s, made for a fun-filled weekend. Included in the group were both Rick Iovine and Gerry Layo, who have joined me on several of my Top 100 excursions. My only complaint for this outing was my arrival with my back out, resulting in too many poor shots and big scores. Next to the Bandon and Pebble resorts, this is my go-to golf resort. For those who have enjoyed Ballybunion in Ireland, Whistling Straits comes with a similar feeling. Outsized mounds and bunkers, this is a picturesque tract on the shores of Lake Michigan. With open, rugged, and windswept terrain, Pete Dye created a true masterpiece here.

22. Blackwolf Run—River: September 6, 2005. Ranked number three on the 2000 Top 100 list, the River tract requires the golfer to be skilled with every club in the bag. It is noted as the most intimidating course in the Midwest, and I could make the case that such a designation could cover a much larger area than that! Giant grassy mounds, vast waste bunkers, kettle-like pot bunkers, split-level fairways, and perched greens defended by huge swales make for all the challenge one could ever ask for. Regardless of the tee boxes played, plan to leave your egos at home. A genuine treat to share with great friends.

23. Bandon Trails: January 20, 2007. The third of the Bandon courses opened in 2005 and regularly ranked in the top twenty. Starts and finishes with massive sand dunes and, in between,

weaves through gorgeous meadows and coastal forests. This tract is quite different than the previous two Bandon courses, and I've heard from many this is their favorite, but I prefer the others. Regardless, it's a great playing experience.

24. Hualalai: June 3, 2008. Racing the Honu 70.3 Ironman brought me to the Big Island, and I was first tee off as a single on this Four Seasons beauty. Generous bright-green fairways, matched against black lava and nestled along a bright-blue Pacific Ocean, sure made for a visual feast. Manicured conditions. My eighty that morning sure made for a great experience.

25. Trump National LA: August 11, 2008. Best friend Rick Iovine and former business partner Brett Dillenberg joined me on this one. Known to be one of the most expensive golf courses ever built at more than $250 million, this Pete Dye–designed beauty is just that! Amazing playing conditions, brilliant white sands, and magnificent ocean views are all part of the experience here. Accuracy is advised, as balls hit off the fairways are most often lost, and penalties mount up quickly. Witness Rick and me at ninety-four and Brett at ninety-six. Regardless, a real *wow* experience.

26. Tobacco Road: July 14, 2013. Built out of the sand hills of North Carolina, here you will find plenty of sandy waste areas. Nonetheless, plenty of safe green fairways set up the player for an enjoyable round. Many will take issue with this assessment; however, I found this course more visually enjoyable than legendary Pinehurst No. 2. Carded an eighty-four that day, adding to my enjoyment.

27. Bethpage Black: August 1, 2014. A sign printed in big red letters is posted behind the first tee: "Warning: The Black Course is an extremely difficult golf course, which is recommended only for highly skilled golfers." This public tract opened in 1936 and has undergone several restorations. Host to several PGA tourneys, this is truly a monster. Tee times often require sleeping out at 4:00 a.m. in hopes of getting on this beast. I was fortunate to have a local friend, Matt Weiss, grab us a tee time without the hassle. (Thank you, Matt!) While our foursome was absent of any good golfers, the scores for the day spoke loudly: 134, 131, 102, and 93. While the numerous bunkers and tight fairways make for tough conditions, playing this classic is a must.

28. Streamsong Red & Blue: December 5–6, 2015. I played the Red as a solo and was joined the next day on the Blue with friend and client Riad Nizam. Located in Florida, about sixty miles out of Tampa, the word to describe these is *unexpected*. Florida courses are generally flat, but at Streamsong you quickly learn that is not the case. Tom Doak, Bill Coore, and Ben Crenshaw have brought that "Bandon Dunes feel" to Florida. Both regularly ranked in the top twenty, these Scottish links call out to be walked for the ideal experience. Undulating fairways, huge bunkers, towering sand dunes, and gnarly greenside pot bunkers are all present. All add up to a fun and challenging experience.

29. Cascata: January 16, 2016. I teamed up with Riad's brother Jamil for this world-class experience just outside of Las Vegas. Carved out of Red Mountain, this is truly target golf. A beautiful conditioned tract inclusive of a natural waterfall and streams throughout, this is a must play when visiting Vegas.

30. Pine Valley: June 5, 2018. Okay, so this amazing course is not
     actually on the Playable Top 100 Golf Courses in the United
     States, and I've played several private courses ranked in their
     own Top 100 and not included in my 100. But when you
     play the number one ranked course in the world, I feel you
     have to include it. (I get to make the rules; after all, it's life
     by design!) A CEO coach client, Tom Londres, found the
     way to get my best friend Rick and me out there for a truly
     magical experience. (Thanks, Tom!) He teamed us up with a
     business partner of his, Glenn Marvin, along with a member
     of the club. Open for play in 1919, the design can only be
     described as *scintillating*. Each hole is unique to itself, and
     rarely can you see another hole from the one you are playing.
     Located just outside of my birthplace, Philadelphia, in the
     sandy pine barrens, this tract is truly demanding. (If you ever
     get the opportunity, check out the drone video of hole-by-
     hole intro, as it will truly help with your survival on the day
     of play.) Relentless bunkers abound, waste bunkers seem to
     be everywhere, and not a rake is to be found on the course.
     Pine Valley requires a high degree of mental toughness—all
     the while you walk in a seeming sense of tranquility, yet
     brutal is a more apt description of the course. Throughout
     the day it seems as if each shot requires a controlled carry
     over sand and water. Rick carded a 98, and I posted a 102,
     and we both felt we played well that day! The club house is
     intentionally understated, and I suspect every visitor picks up
     their fair share of memory logo wear. We sure did!

In a cursory review of the list at the beginning of this appendix,
you can see that by the year 2008, I had knocked down eighty of

the Top 100, keeping my pace for an initially desired completion in a ten-year period. However, it would be five years before I played another for number eighty-one. In 2007 I got bit by the Ironman triathlon bug, and squeezing in both sports along with business, travel, and home life demanded that something had to give. As such, it would take me eight years to pick up the next fifteen on my list. Life holds forth so many opportunities, but at the end of the day, we are all maxed at twenty-four hours a day. Accordingly, when designing one's life, it's about trade-offs. But remember—we get to decide! Given the choice, I would highly recommend this golf journey as a genuinely fun bucket list entry.

As mentioned earlier, it was my intent to play my "final five" the year before I wrote this book, but during the first half of 2020, I battled a severed quad tendon surgery and malignant melanoma surgery (proclaimed cancer-free), and the world challenged a pandemic. Be assured that my life design is calling out for one hundred!

PRESIDENTIAL LIBRARIES JOURNEY

1. William Clinton #42 3/4/2006

    Little Rock, AR

2. John Kennedy #35 4/16/2007; 4/23/2014; 4/2015

    Boston, MA

3. Gerald Ford #38 10/8/2009; 5/1/2015

    Grand Rapids, MI

4. Lyndon Johnson #36 10/23/2009

    Austin, TX

5. Jimmy Carter #39 5/23/13; 3/20/2016

    Atlanta, GA

6. Ronald Reagan #40 12/16/2013; 8/25/2014; 9/5/2015

    Simi Valley, CA

7. Dwight Eisenhower #34 4/11/2014

    Abilene, KS

8. George W. Bush #43 12/8/2014

    Dallas, TX

9. George H. W. Bush #41 12/14/2014

   College Station, TX

10. Franklin Roosevelt #32 5/16/2015

    Hyde Park, NY

11. Richard Nixon #37 5/18/15; 2/2/2019; 4/5/2019

    Yorba Linda, CA

12. Harry Truman #33 12/11/2015

    Independence, MO

13. Herbert Hoover #31 7/15/2016

    West Branch, IA

OTHER NOTABLES:

1. George Washington / Mount Vernon 6/22/2014

2. Johnson Ranch 8/18/2015

3. 9/11 Museum 8/2/2014

4. West Point 12/5/2014

5. Pentagon 3/11/2015

6. Air Force Academy 8/16/2015

7. CIA 5/18/2016

APPENDIX 9: MORE PIVOTAL MOMENTS

Included here are a few more pivotal stories in my life that didn't make the "meat" of the book but are nonetheless important and represent valuable life lessons and experiences.

CART BOY

At seventeen years old, I answered a job posting seeking a cart boy for a newly opened grocery store. I was offered the job and quickly discovered there were twelve cart boys hired to handle the store opening, with search lights shining in the air and many specials with free food or deeply discounted food to lure new shoppers. The store was an anchor property to a large shopping mall, where carts would be dispersed throughout. I quickly assessed that once the lights and freebies were removed, the need for twelve cart boys would be gone, and one or two would likely make the cut. Since the union pay was higher than anything else out there, I committed to being one of the "survivors." I made the effort into a game, always ensuring that I would get the store manager's attention with my hustle. That approach worked, and I became one of the two "survivors."

I decided that a consistency of such a work ethic would likely reap rewards, so I continued with my hustle, and whenever something needed to be done, I would be the volunteer. Mitch

Saffron was the relatively young store manager, and Mitch took notice. Eventually, he told me to pick my hours, as many as I wanted and whatever days I would like, since I would be doing more than any of the other two hundred employees at the store, whatever I was doing. This led to my being named assistant store manager in my late teens, thereby learning the business importance of hiring, firing, and leading people to improved performance. The store was one of the top-performing stores in the large chain, and I learned that the magic of Mitch was creating a culture of winners, bolstered by recognition and rewards. These were principles that would serve me well in my life by design.

CFO

In my early thirties, I held the position of CFO / SVP of administration for a national company. I reported to the CEO, a man named Jon Tilley. One day Tilley called me into his office and declared me to be his hardest-working direct report. Following this compliment, he then asked if I ever had given thought as to where I wanted to go in life. I laughed at his question and went on to share with him the story of my four categories of goals set at thirteen years old, one of which was to be the CEO of a national company in the money business. Now, here I was in just such a company; the only problem was he was in his early forties, and he had my job! We both laughed, and Jon went on to make a commitment for a succession plan, and one day soon, if necessary, he would leave the company and hand me the keys.

However, he noted I needed more experience in a few key areas. I suggested he transfer me over to those positions, and he declined, as he didn't want me out of my present role. I mentioned it would be impossible for me to learn the other roles, as mine was already a full-time endeavor. Jon then proposed that I take two weeks additional vacation, with both weeks back to back. Further, those weeks were to be the last week of the month and the first week of the next month. This was a big ask, as the last week was when we closed the books and the first week was when financial statements were produced. Additionally, during those two weeks, I was forbidden to be in touch with my accounting team. Upon return, I would discover that the books were indeed closed and financials produced. For the next three months, I had to commit to staying away from the accounting area for those same two weeks and learn the areas in which I was weak.

I'm proud to report that the team stepped up and delivered the financials, and I was able to learn the areas where I was weakest. Not long after that, Jon knocked on my office door, threw the keys to the business to me, and headed off to Wall Street. Lessons learned were once again the importance of knowing what you want in life (intention/vision/goals) and the power of delegation and trusting others to perform.

ARTHUR ANDERSEN

When I graduated from university as an accounting major, I went to work for Arthur Andersen, known as a Big Eight accounting firm at the time. By then, I was not only married but also dad to our daughter, Melissa. While I was moving along quickly in the firm, my schedule was nearly 100 percent out-of-town travel. When I found the company unwilling to make changes so I could spend time with my family (while there were single employees with 100 percent nontraveling assignments), I decided to find another opportunity. I quickly snared a bigger-title position with a considerable increase in income while being able to be home each evening.

That sure sounded good; however, the commute was an hour each way, and the work could be done in 20 percent of the time. Within a year I elected to leave to more of an entrepreneurial opportunity, which led to a decade-long business journey. The lesson I learned here, which I have shared with many over the years, is whenever making career decisions, be sure you are "going to something that is in line with your passions, as opposed to leaving something." I left Arthur Andersen to "leave" and did not do my due diligence that I was pursuing something I would be passionate about.

MASTERMIND GROUPS

One of the important contributors to my life by design is participating in mastermind groups. This is where regular gatherings of individuals share success stories, share challenges they are encountering, and overall come together to assist one another in their pursuits of well-lived lives. I've had the pleasure of such interactions in groups such as TEC/Vistage, YPO, EO, GOT, and several other smaller groups. The list of people who have positively impacted my life pursuits is too lengthy to list, but I encourage all to seek out such opportunities.

APPENDIX 10: COPY OF TRACKING CALENDAR PAGE

APPENDIX 11: BLANK TEMPLATES TO CREATE YOUR LIFE BY DESIGN

Note: This book is also available in an audio format without the appendices. The appendices can be accessed on the websites www.jackdalysales.com and www.jackdalyslifebydesign.com.

STEP 1: BIG QUESTIONS:

1. What do I want in my life?

   _____

   _____

2. Why do I want it?

   _____

   _____

3. When do I want it by?

   _____

   _____

4. What do I choose to do in order to achieve it?

   _____

   _____

STEP 2: WHERE ARE YOU NOW?

HEALTH/FITNESS:

1. How would I rate my overall health on a scale of 1–10?

   _____

   _____

2. Am I taking care of myself, generally speaking?

   _____

   _____

3. How much time am I allotting each week to this area of my life?

   _____

   _____

4. Am I getting sufficient sleep?

   _____

   _____

5. Am I following a healthy eating plan?

   _____

   _____

6. What are some initial ideas to improve in this area?

   _____

   _____

FAMILY:

1. On a scale of 1–10, how do I rate my relationship with my spouse/significant other?

   _____

   _____

2. On a scale of 1–10, how do I rate my relationship with my children?

   _____

   _____

3. On a scale of 1–10, how do I rate my more distant family relationships?

   _____

   _____

4. What are the strengths in my relationship with my spouse/ significant other?

   _____

   _____

5. What are the areas that can be improved with my spouse/ significant other?

   _____

   _____

6. What are the strengths in my relationship with my children?

   _____

   _____

7. What are the areas that can be improved with my children?

_____

_____

FINANCIAL:

1. Do I have a financial plan for my family life?

_____

_____

2. Do I operate with a monthly budget?

_____

_____

3. Do I have an age for desired retirement?

_____

_____

4. Have I determined the amount of money needed for retirement?

_____

_____

5. Do I have specific income goals?

_____

_____

6. Do I have debt?

_____

_____

7. If in debt, do I have a plan to retire such debt?

_____

_____

8. Am I adequately insured? In what way?

_____

_____

LEISURE:

1. Do I have a desire to read? If so, how often?

_____

_____

2. Do I enjoy movies? If so, how often?

_____

_____

3. What are typical activities spent with the family?

_____

_____

4. What kind of vacations have I been taking?

_____

_____

5. Do I have a plan for vacations?

_____

_____

6. Do I have a bucket list? For myself? For family?

_____

_____

7. What about family meals together? Frequency?

_____

_____

8. What are the things I've done with leisure time that provided me the greatest satisfaction?

_____

_____

SPORT:

1. What sports do I enjoy as a spectator?

_____

_____

2. What sports do I enjoy participating in?

_____

_____

3. How often do I participate in desired sports?

_____

_____

4. What sports would I enjoy playing but have yet to carve the time out for?

_____

_____

SPIRITUAL:

1. On a scale of 1–10, how important is this area in my life?

_____

_____

2. On a scale of 1–10, how would I assess my participation here?

_____

_____

3. How would I describe my spiritual life today?

_____

_____

4. What could I improve upon in this area?

_____

_____

GROWTH:

1. On a scale of 1–10, how would I assess myself in this area?

   _____

   _____

2. What activities have I done in this area?

   _____

   _____

3. What activities would I like to see more of?

   _____

   _____

4. What percent of activity is tied to my profession?

   _____

   _____

5. What percent of activity is tied to my personal life?

   _____

   _____

BUSINESS/CAREER:

1. How would I categorize the time I have invested in my profession?

   _____

   _____

2. What businesses/roles have I worked in?

_____

_____

3. On a scale of 1–10, how would I rate my happiness in this area?

_____

_____

4. What would be needed to raise that happiness number?

_____

_____

5. Where is my passion when it comes to career?

_____

_____

6. What stands in the way of improvement here?

_____

_____

FRIENDS:

1. List the names of some old friends.

_____

_____

2. List the names of some new friends.

    _____

    _____

3. How often do I get together with these friends?

    _____

    _____

4. Are these get-togethers in person or over the phone?

    _____

    _____

5. Is this the desired mix of friends and frequency?

    _____

    _____

6. Do I feel I have too many or too few, or is the mix about right?

    _____

    _____

7. What could I change to improve this area of my life?

    _____

    _____

STEP 3: VALUES & TASKS

List twelve or more things you value most. Don't worry about the order or priority; at this stage it's about quantity, not quality.

1. _____   11. _____

2. _____   12. _____

3. _____   13. _____

4. _____   14. _____

5. _____   15. _____

6. _____   16. _____

7. _____   17. _____

8. _____   18. _____

9. _____   19. _____

10. _____   20. _____

Now, review the above listing, and circle the top three most important to you.

TASK LISTS

Once you've identified your top three values, create task lists that you would need to complete to successfully integrate these three values into your life.

MOST IMPORTANT VALUE: _____

To-do list:

a) _____

b) _____

c) _____

d) _____

e) _____

f) _____

g) _____

After you have completed the list for your most important value, then move on to the second value, and then complete the third using the same process.

IMPORTANT VALUE: _____

To-do list:

a) _____

b) _____

c) _____

d) _____

e) _____

f) _____

g) _____

IMPORTANT VALUE: _____

To-do list:

    a) _____

    b) _____

    c) _____

    d) _____

    e) _____

    f) _____

    g) _____

STEP 4: LIFETIME GOALS & TASKS

Next, we move to more of a goal-setting process, listing goals you hope to achieve in your lifetime. Consider what you would like to achieve in your lifetime, and list your lifetime goals. As with your values, it's more about quantity than quality, and the ordering is not important at this stage. There is no right number of goals to include here; you need to determine what feels right for you.

1. _____   11. _____

2. _____   12. _____

3. _____   13. _____

4. _____   14. _____

5. _____   15. _____

6. _____   16. _____

7. _____   17. _____

8. _____   18. _____

9. _____   19. _____

10. _____   20. _____

Now, circle the top three from your list. Following the same process as with the values, create a task list for your top three goals.

MOST IMPORTANT GOAL: _____

To-do list:

a) _____

b) _____

c) _____

d) _____

e) _____

f) _____

g) _____

Complete the process with each of your top three goals.

IMPORTANT GOAL: _____

To-do list:

a) _____

b) _____

c) _____

d) _____

e) _____

f) _____

g) _____

IMPORTANT GOAL: _____

To-do list:

a) _____

b) _____

c) _____

d) _____

e) _____

f) _____

g) _____

STEP 5: FIVE-YEAR GOALS & TASKS

Now we want to bring the goals into a near-term focus. Following a now-familiar process, list your near-term goals, those you'd like to achieve in the next five years. Once again, it's more about quantity than quality, and the ordering is not important at this stage, and the number of goals that is right is determined by you.

1. _____ 11. _____

2. _____ 12. _____

3. _____ 13. _____

4. _____ 14. _____

5. _____ 15. _____

6. _____ 16. _____

7. _____   17. _____

8. _____   18. _____

9. _____   19. _____

10. _____   20. _____

Circle the top three from the above listing. As before, run your top three through the task-list process.

MOST IMPORTANT GOAL: _____

To-do list:

a) _____

b) _____

c) _____

d) _____

e) _____

f) _____

g) _____

Complete this for each of your top three five-year goals.

IMPORTANT GOAL: _____

To-do list:

a) _____

b) _____

c) _____

d) _____

e) _____

f) _____

g) _____

IMPORTANT GOAL: _____

To-do list:

a) _____

b) _____

c) _____

d) _____

e) _____

f) _____

g) _____

STEP 6: SIX-MONTH GOALS & TASKS

If you only had six months to live, how would you spend them? List your near-term, immediate goals. Again, it's more about quantity than quality, and the ordering is not important at this stage.

1. _____   11. _____

2. _____   12. _____

3. _____   13. _____

4. _____   14. _____

5. _____   15. _____

6. _____   16. _____

7. _____   17. _____

8. _____   18. _____

9. _____   19. _____

10. _____   20. _____

Circle the top three and run them through the task-list process.

MOST IMPORTANT GOAL: _____

To-do list:

a) _____

b) _____

c) _____

d) _____

e) _____

f) _____

g) _____

IMPORTANT GOAL: _____

To-do list:

a) _____

b) _____

c) _____

d) _____

e) _____

f) _____

g) _____

IMPORTANT GOAL: _____

To-do list:

a) _____

b) _____

c) _____

d) _____

e) _____

f) _____

g) _____

STEP 7: THE BUCKET LIST

MY BEGINNING BUCKET LIST

1. _____

2. _____

3. _____

4. _____

5. _____

6. _____

7. _____

8. _____

9. _____

10. _____

11. _____

12. _____

13. _____

14. _____

15. _____

16. _____

17. _____

18. _____

19. _____

20. _____

21. _____

22. _____

STEP 8: ONE-YEAR PLAN

Annual plan: This rough outline should be tailored to fit *your* goals.

PERSONAL GOALS:

_____

_____

_____

_____

_____

THEME:

_____

_____

_____

_____

_____

A. _____

    1. _____

    2. _____

    3. _____

    4. _____

B. _____

    1. _____

    2. _____

    3. _____

    4. _____

C. _____

    1. _____

    2. _____

    3. _____

    4. _____

CRYSTAL BALL

Step 1: Describe the year ahead based on the crystal ball's prediction. _____ year has come and gone, and we "rocked" because we achieved the following specific and measurable *outcomes*.

    1. _____

    2. _____

    3. _____

4. _____

5. _____

6. _____

Step 2: What are the top five or six specific and measurable things that made it such a great year? Rank them in order. These are the *activities* that led to the result in step 1.

1. _____

2. _____

3. _____

4. _____

5. _____

6. _____

Note: *This book is also available in an audio format without the appendices. The appendices can be accessed on the websites www.jackdalysales.com and www.jackdalyslifebydesign.com.*

Oct 1994 marked Bonnie and I completing our first
marathons in Portland, Oregon.

I completed my 50th state marathon in New Jersey in
April 2018, supported by friends and family.

My first Rim2Rim at Grand Canyon shared with Rick Iovine in March 2009, high temps hit 115 degrees.

I gifted my Life Mentor Jim Pratt with the first copy of Amazon #1 Best Seller *Hyper Sales Growth* March 2014. June of 2020 set Guinness World Record.

In May of 2018 ran the Great Wall Marathon for my last of 7 continent marathons. Shared with Rick Iovine as he ran the Half Marathon.

Finished my first Ironman in the United Kingdom in
August 2007 with a time of 14:51.

Bonnie and I traveled to India in June 2008.
The Taj Mahal was one of many highlights.

In September of 2008 I joined prized client Laticrete for
a week of world renowned golf and friendship.

Second quarter 2018 notable life accomplishments.

Bonnie and I hiked the trails into Machu Picchu in July 2011 and I returned in March 2017 with Rick Iovine.

In September 2001 Bonnie and I climbed the Sydney Bridge, one of many highlights of our visits to Australia.

Sister Valerie joined me in racing her first Ironman in Cozumel in November 2010. Great to have so many family members there to support us.

52 years to the day after meeting Bonnie I ran the NYC
Marathon on November 5, 2017, raising a record $200k+
for the Jimmy Valvano Foundation fighting cancer.

January 2008 family and friends joined in Orlando
to run the Goofy (marathon and half marathon
back-to-back days).

August 2006 took on the world's first and highest bungee jumps in New Zealand. In April 2017, Wei Chen enabled my flying a jet fighter plane.

Garnered 3rd place in my age group in Ironman South Africa in April 2011 with a 13:19 finish.

My first visit to Israel in November 2019 included many incredible moments. Karen and I visiting the Western Wall in Jerusalem was jaw-dropping.